INDUSTRIAL ORGANIZATION

PRINCIPLES OF ECONOMICS SERIES

under the editorship of

EDWARD AMES

INDUSTRIAL ORGANIZATION
An Empirical Approach

STANLEY E. BOYLE

VIRGINIA POLYTECHNIC INSTITUTE AND STATE UNIVERSITY

Holt, Rinehart and Winston, Inc.

NEW YORK   CHICAGO   SAN FRANCISCO   ATLANTA

DALLAS   MONTREAL   TORONTO   LONDON   SYDNEY

14-5597

EDITOR'S FOREWORD

One of the oldest and most topical questions discussed by economists has been that of competition and monopoly. Our earliest image of the monopolist—that of the man at the oasis collecting astronomical fees from thirsty desert travelers—has been greatly modified by our knowledge of modern industry, where mixtures of competitive and monopolistic elements are the rule. Professor Boyle here has systematized a large body of findings to introduce the questions: In what parts of the economy are monopolistic elements strongest? What evidence is there to show strengthening or weakening of competition in recent decades? and, What instruments of corporate policy seem to be effective in strengthening monopoly power?

This volume is one of a series of short introductions to important topics in modern economics. The publishers and the editor have been impressed by the development of economic research over the past twenty years, and by the slowness with which many exciting new problems have become accessible to undergraduates and their teachers. It is not yet apparent which parts of this new research will become the backbone of teaching programs of the future, but it is clear that important changes will occur. The publication of a series of short, paperback volumes will permit instructors to experiment with new course material in areas where existing subject matter seems dated. Such a series also encourages the participation of young and active scholars in the development of new course material, without forcing them to write long textbook manuscripts. The series as a whole is designed to present a balanced presentation of new and traditional course material in such a way as to make it easier for instructors to introduce their students to the leading ideas and methods of modern economic thought.

Stony Brook, New York   Edward Ames
December 1971

PREFACE

The systematic analysis of the problems encompassed in the field of industrial organization is a rather recent development. In part, it is an outgrowth of the continuing inability of formal economic theory (competitive and monopolistic) to provide specific solutions to the problems which have arisen concerning changes in competitive conditions in actual markets over the past few decades. Renewed efforts were made during the 1930s to understand the conditions responsible for the downturn in economic activity. The concurrent publication of *The Theory of Monopolistic Competition* represented an effort to apply formal microeconomic theory to these problems. Over the past 20 years, efforts to solve these problems have been intensified. In this, as in many other areas, a limited number of individuals have taken the lead in the development of both the theoretical concepts and the analytical tools with which progress can be made. That is certainly true in the field of industrial organization. Many of the "new" and important developments which have been made in recent years have come from one man, Joe S. Bain. Many others have been inspired by him. In a real sense, this book and all others on this subject owe an immeasurable debt to the insight and innovative skill of Professor Bain.

This book is designed to assist the beginning student in economics possessing little more than the basic microeconomic principles in applying his limited knowledge of economics to an understanding of the problems which the complex industry structures of today have fostered.

It seeks to provide the student with a framework which will enable him to *understand* the importance of the changes in industry conditions which have occurred and to make meaningful criticisms of decisions, both private and public, which affect the structure and performance of U.S. firms here and abroad. These are not abstract and immaterial considerations. They affect the economic well-being of every citizen of this country every day of his life. They determine the type and variety of products which are available, their cost, and even the terms of sale. *They are vital.*

The typical textbook references to the structure and performance of firms in imperfectly competitive industries are sterile. They suggest in a rather general manner that a range of possible types of behavior may exist in imperfectly competitive industries, but do not indicate, however, how and with what data these conclusions are actually reached. Nor do they indicate the probable competitive significance of these conclusions. It may be felt that this is too complex a set of problems to thrust upon a relative beginner in the field. Yet the author feels most strongly that those who adhere to such beliefs both flatter the depths of their knowledge and their conception of the complexity of the field and, moreover, insult the intelligence of the student.

With this point of view and a three-fold purpose in mind, the approach adopted in this book is one of incorporating as much empirical information as possible into the basic theoretical framework firstly, by imparting to the student some understanding of the application of basic microeconomic theory of the firm to imperfectly competitive industries; secondly, by indicating the actual processes which have been or might be followed in obtaining empirical results which are both sensible and meaningful; and thirdly, by arousing in the student, through brief discussions of the limitations of the available data, a healthy skepticism of all "facts" and obvious "solutions" proposed by professionals working in this or any other area. Truth is a commodity with a very short life.

It is the author's belief that books in this and other areas of economics have talked too much about general methods of approach without examining and explaining the complex and sometimes nasty problems inherent in developing data and finding solutions. The present book does not attempt to provide the student with an abbreviated course in antitrust law, however tempting the opportunity. The actions by Congress in enhancing and reducing the acceptable scope of competition on a case-by-case basis over the past 70 years is too tortured to attempt to explain in a chapter or two. I am the first to admit that I am unable to provide clarity to an area which has suffered from Congressional and judicial confusion for about 80 years.

The book opens with a general introduction to some of the more pressing problems faced in the area of industrial organization economics, including a brief discussion of some important terminology. The next two chapters are devoted to an examination of the major structural characteristics of U.S. industry. In some instances, suggestions are included which may explain major changes that have occurred. Attention is devoted in succeeding chapters to the conduct of firms in imperfectly competitive industries and the resulting economic performance of such industries. Chapter 6 contains three brief case studies: synthetic rubber, bakery products, and automotive tires. These studies are designed to depict the relationship of industry structure to conduct and performance in a few actual industry situations. The final chapter relates contemporary economic analysis to the solution of antitrust problems. This does not include an extended discussion of the laws themselves. Instead it discusses the role of economics and economists in providing answers to the full range of antitrust problems which exist. This role is one of considerable importance and one which is often misunderstood by the economist and the lawyer alike. The magnitude of the gulf between these two professions is nowhere clearer than in the actual practice of antitrust litigation.

In large part, this book is the result of the author's experience as an economist with the Antitrust Division of the Department of Justice and as Chief, Division of Industry Analysis, Federal Trade Commission. My former colleagues in those agencies have shared in the development of the ideas which are incorporated in this book. They are to be absolved of all blame for any errors which remain.

My last and largest debt which must be acknowledged is to my wife, who encouraged me to undertake this venture and who managed to retain her good humor when all seemed lost.

Blacksburg, Virginia   Stanley E. Boyle
December 1971

CONTENTS

INDUSTRIAL ORGANIZATION

1

THE PROBLEM AND THE SETTING

Microeconomic theory provides a clear and basic framework within which to present models of competitive and monopolistic industrial behavior. Given the limiting structural conditions of these two market forms, it is possible to *predict* with considerable accuracy the resultant performance of firms (enterprises) in response to basic changes in industry supply and demand. The simplicity and clarity of the formal solutions in these two market structures may well mislead those unfamiliar with the problems inherent in imperfectly competitive industries to assume that simple and clean solutions are possible in all types of market structure. That is not true.

You have already learned that there is only a limited number of industries that meet the necessary structural conditions of the perfectly competitive industry: many buyers and sellers, homogeneous products, and ease of entry and exit. Aside from the production of raw materials (agriculture, coal mining, and forestry) examples of industries that meet all three conditions are difficult to develop. Similarly, the economist is usually hard pressed to suggest good examples for the classic conception of a perfectly monopolized industry. The local telephone company, the local electric utility, Western Union, and the Aluminum Company of America (Alcoa) prior to World War II are some examples that come to mind readily, and they are used quite often. However, these examples are not particularly interesting from an analytical point of view. The first three, for example, are subject to Federal and State price and profit

1

regulation. Consequently, they serve as monuments to the failure of competition and cannot be used as good examples of private monopoly. Alcoa lost its monopoly position in the production of virgin ingot aluminum in the United States as the result of the sale of the government-financed aluminum plants built during World War II to Reynolds and Kaiser.

A few minutes' reflection is sufficient to understand why very few major industries exhibit the necessary structural conditions to warrant classification as monopolistic or perfectly competitive industries. For example, the production of automobiles does not fit the standard economic model of the competitive industry with many producers, homogeneous products, and ease of entry. Nor, for that matter, does it fit the case of a perfect monopoly. The same could be said of most of the other products you see every day. Most important consumer products originate in industries with only a few producers—automobiles, television and radio sets, electric and gas appliances, hard-surface floor coverings, alcoholic beverages, sporting goods, children's wheeled vehicles and dolls are but a few examples.

The basic analytical models—competition and monopoly—are not directly usable in the analysis or appraisal of the conduct and behavior of firms in an imperfectly competitive industry. They do, however, provide a point of departure, which may assist in answering many of the questions that are important for an appraisal of the operation of an industry: Is the present size distribution of firms in an industry consistent with that necessary to achieve maximum efficiency? Is there a most efficient-sized firm? What factors determine the optimum-size firm? What is the optimum level of competition, measured in terms of the number of firms, attainable in an industry? Would competition be enhanced by an increase (decrease) in the number of firms in an industry? Are optimum competition and economic efficiency conflicting goals? Does economic theory have anything to say about any of these questions?

As esoteric as these questions may seem to you, they have real world counterparts. The Federal Trade Commission and the Antitrust Division of the Department of Justice have been entrusted by the Congress with the enforcement of statutes which seek, for the most part, to forestall the development of uncompetitive industry structures and to restrict certain types of anticompetitive behavior by firms in our economy. It is their general responsibility to discourage actions by firms, singly or in concert with others, which may result in the monopolization of industries. Specifically, they seek to forestall attempts by groups of firms to set prices, allocate markets, and limit the entry of new firms. Much of their current energy is devoted to the elimination of mergers which may have the actual or potential effect of restricting competition in a market.

Their responsibility is impossibly broad and demanding. They are charged with the maintenance of competition and the elimination of the activities which tend to diminish competition, throughout the major portion of our economy. (Some notable exceptions are discussed in the final chapter.) Assuming for the moment that they are interested in performing their assigned tasks in as conscientious a manner as possible, antitrust cases become an arena in which the basic structural and performance relationships are tested and analyzed. The organization of an industry, its structure and performance, become the primary substantive issues of interest in the area of antitrust.

SOME BASIC TERMINOLOGY

In this, as in almost every other specialized area of knowledge, there are terms which take on particular and sometimes very specific meanings. Some of these terms are already familiar to you in a general sense, others may be considerably less familiar. Six terms (industry, product, market, structure, conduct, and performance) are used repeatedly throughout this book. As a consequence, attention is devoted to their meaning and use at this time. Other terms will be introduced as they are needed in subsequent chapters.

Industry An industry is composed of a group of establishments engaged primarily in the same or closely related types of business activity. Manufacturing industries, for example, are described in terms of either the production process employed or the product produced. In wholesale and retail trade, they are defined in terms of the sales method employed or the nature of products sold. On the surface, it might appear that each distinct product should be considered a separate industry. In practice, however, such a classification scheme would be most impractical, resulting in thousands of different industry classifications.

What does determine the bounds of an industry? The Bureau of the Census, and others engaged in the collection and publication of production data, attempt to conform to some fundamental notion of an industry which is theoretically defensible but which incorporates a variety of practical considerations. Some of these considerations are revealed in this statement:

> One of the main purposes of industry classification is to facilitate the compilation of data describing the magnitude and characteristics of the country's economic activity in an orderly manner and in terms of a manageable number of meaningful categories.[1]

[1] Maxwell R. Conklin and Harold T. Goldstein, "Census Principles of Industry and Product Classification, Manufacturing Industries," *Business Concentration and Price Policy*, National Bureau of Economic Research, Princeton (1955), p. 17.

4 *The Problem and the Setting*

Ideally, an industry includes all establishments engaged in provision of the same type of service or the production of similar product classes. Using this basic scheme, the *1967 Census of Manufactures* classified the output of all manufacturing establishments in the United States into 417 industries.[2] As a consequence, data related to value complicates the analysis of changes in the structure of particular industries, but it does not eliminate the usefulness of the concept in the economic analysis of firm conduct and performance.

Product   An industry includes a variety of product classes and obviously an even wider collection of individual products. Thus, in contrast with the general nature of the concept of industry, a *product* is a precise classification—roasted coffee, whole bean (20951 11); roasted coffee, ground (20951 15), and the like.

Extensive product information is both time-consuming and costly to collect. Consequently, its collection is undertaken only in the *Census of Manufactures*.[3] On the other hand, industry data has been collected annually since 1949, and appears in the *Annual Survey of Manufactures*.

Market   Ours is sometimes referred to as a market economy without particular attention to the meaning of the word. Basically, a market includes all the competing sellers and buyers of a particular product or set of products. The market has then at least two important dimensions: a product and a geographic area. For example, the market for bread or bakery products, milk and most milk products, newspapers, beverages, concrete products, and cement, is relatively small and localized. In these cases, production and consumption tends to take place in a limited geographic area. A small bakery in California is obviously not in the same market as a bakery in Vermont. They do not have common customers. They are not competitors. On the other hand, many geographic markets are nation-wide in scope. Such markets include motor vehicles, ciga-

[2] The industry is one of the concepts embodied in the Standard Industrial Classification system (SIC). The degree of classification is indicated by the number of digits shown. For example:

SIC	CLASSIFICATION	TITLE
27	Major Industry Group	Printing and Publishing
273	Industry Group	Books
2731	Industry	Books: Publishing and Printing
27311	Product Class	Textbooks
27311–16	Product	College textbooks, paperbound

The most comprehensive listing of Census classifications is to be found in the *Numerical List of Manufactured Products* which is published by the Bureau of the Census. Since World War II it has appeared in 1947, 1954, 1958, 1963, and 1967.

[3] During the postwar period, complete *Censuses of Manufactures* were made in 1947, 1954, 1958, 1963, and 1967.

rettes, clothing, refined petroleum products, paper products, footwear and toys. Producers of these products, irrespective of their location in the country, may well have the same customers (particularly retail chain stores which sell nation-wide) and compete with one another.

The sellers' side of the market conforms, in most respects, to our earlier description of an industry. It goes beyond this to include the buyers' side as well, since the number, size, and geographic distribution of buyers influences the behavior of sellers. Both groups—buyers and sellers —interact upon one another to produce market results. Moreover, variations on the buyers' side of the market may be as important in determining the competitive conduct of firms as that of the sellers' side. Thus, both must be included.

Structure   Much of the effort of economists interested in industrial organization has been devoted to the definition and measurement of the structural characteristics of markets or industries. Here we mean those factors that will determine the form and nature of the conduct and performance of firms in given industries. Some of the more important structural variables have already been mentioned: the number, relative size, and geographic distribution of buyers and sellers.

Why is the structure of a market or industry of particular concern to us? The answer to this question is simple. Economic theory suggests that the particular structural form of an industry *determines* the type of conduct and performance that will prevail. If the number of sellers is relatively small but the number of buyers is large, sellers may have substantial control over the determination of prices and competitive strategy employed. Conversely, if the number of sellers is large and the number of buyers is relatively small, economic power may well reside with the buyers, with sellers exerting little, if any, control over price.

There is a substantial number of structural characteristics which are important in the analysis of market conditions. The most important of these are described below.

1. The *degree of concentration* shows the number and size distribution of *buyers and sellers* in any given market. The degree of concentration, both buyer and seller, is probably the most important structural characteristic.

2. *Change in the size of the market* refers to the relative growth of the output and sales of the industry, not to its geographic size. Is it an expanding industry? For example, many contend that rapid increases in industry size tend to offset the effects of high levels of concentration.

3. The *degree of product differentiation* is the extent to which buyers consider the outputs of various sellers in the market as being different. These differences may be *real* or *imagined*. For example, almost all liquid bleaches sold in grocery stores contain a $5\frac{1}{4}\%$ hyperchlorite solu-

tion. Put another way, they are all chemically identical. As a result of extensive promotional activity, some brands (principally Clorox and Purex) are sold at prices in excess of those charged for other brands. Thus, some buyers have been convinced that they are different from other liquid bleaches. The success of such efforts can be measured by the magnitude of the price differentials between brands of similar products in the market. The extent of such activities can be measured by the size of the expenditures made on promotional activities.

4. The *condition of entry* refers to the relative ease or difficulty with which new firms may enter an industry. The condition is usually appraised in terms of the cost advantages which existing firms in a market have over prospective entrants. If conditions of entry are unfavorable (barriers to entry are high), then the competitive effect of entry upon existing firms by potential entrants is limited. Stated in another way, this means that new or prospective entrants may be unable to obtain a share of industry sales which is sufficient for them to become viable competitors. On the other hand, favorable entry conditions, low barriers to entry, may mean that potential entrants are able to exert considerable competitive pressure upon established sellers.

Thus far, attention has been directed to a limited list of *major* structural characteristics that condition the conduct and performance of firms. Obviously, there are others. However, the reader should have been impressed at this early point with the fact that there is no simple or easy combination of structural factors that yield an absolutely predictable mode of behavior. With the exception of those which are characterized by perfect competition (no monopoly) no two markets have identical structures, and no two will behave in the same way. Consequently, the structure of each industry may well require individual analysis if meaningful and intelligent conclusions are to be reached with respect to competitive conditions in it.

Conduct   The market conduct of firms encompasses the range of responses they may make to the structure (or changes in the structure) of the markets in which they operate, and to the actions of their competitors. These five basic conduct characteristics suggest the limit and scope of the conduct referred to.

1. *The objectives of the firm in adopting a price policy.* Do firms attempt to maximize individual firm profits? Do they attempt some form of joint (industry-wide) profit maximization? Do they attempt some sort of target-return pricing? Or do they follow some form of sales maximization policy?

2. *The method employed in achieving this objective.* Does this mean a single-price industry-wide system or some form of discriminatory pric-

ing? Do firms attempt to minimize the number of price changes through time or do prices reflect basic changes in market conditions? Do some or all major firms engage in some form of price discrimination?

3. *The product policy of firms.* What is the firm's policy toward product variation through time? In the automotive industry, for example, some have claimed that rapid style changes by the major U.S. automobile producers is one of the basic reasons for the forced departure of a number of the smaller and financially less viable automobile producers over the past 20 years.

4. *The promotional policy of firms.* What role does advertising play in the overall market strategy of the firm in imperfectly competitive markets? What type of promotional practices are typically employed? How do firms make their decisions regarding the magnitude and distribution of expenditures between products and media?

5. *The overall means of coordination adopted to achieve these goals.* Do firms in the industry follow a practice of complete independence in their decision making? Do they participate in some form of "tacit" interdependent behavior with other firms in the industry? Do they actively participate in "overt" collusive arrangements with some or all of the firms in their market?

This limited list of conduct characteristics merely suggests the wide range of options open to firms in adjusting to the structure of the market(s) in which they operate. Our interest is in determining whether or not systematic patterns of conduct are associated with specific structural conditions.

Performance   In some ultimate sense, the structure of a market and the conduct of firms in reacting to these structural conditions must be appraised in terms of an industry's performance. We are interested in the extent to which the results obtained in a market correspond to or deviate from those which might be expected in a competitive market. This does not mean that all departures from competitive norms are necessarily bad. It does mean, however, that it is useful to identify those dimensions of firm and industry performance which can be appraised in terms of competitive norms. If actual performance deviates too far from the norm, then concern is justifiable.

Some of the major performance dimensions which have been identified and measured include the following:

1. *Long-run cost-price differentials.* By this we mean the presence of long-run profits which appear to exceed those which can be expected, based on the cost of capital, the risk involved, and returns in other economic pursuits.

2. *The progressiveness of the industry.* The rate of new product development and the rate at which new or improved production techniques are applied.
3. *The long-run presence of substantial unused production capacity.* The presence of persistent excess capacity in an industry may affect the competitive behavior of firms in that market.

Questions regarding the operation of an industry must always be answered in terms of the results obtained. Does industry performance conform to that which might be desired as a matter of public policy, *or* does it depart from the optimum to such an extent that governmental action must be taken to remedy the results? The analytical process involved in making this determination necessarily involves the ability to identify, measure, and appraise the salient characteristics of structure and conduct. In this way, if remedial action is necessary it can be adapted to the particular problems which exist in that industry. To some extent, therefore, the analysis and approach must be designed to fit each situation.

We are not entirely in the dark in analyzing these problems. Economic theory suggests that certain specific market structures and methods of conduct will result in "desirable" performance. On the other hand, other types will give "undesirable" results. Since information relating to the structure of markets and the conduct of firms is more amenable to measurement than are performance variables, primary emphasis has been placed there. We assume the causal relationship to run in the direction shown.

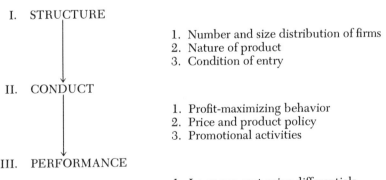

I. STRUCTURE

        1. Number and size distribution of firms
        2. Nature of product
        3. Condition of entry

II. CONDUCT

        1. Profit-maximizing behavior
        2. Price and product policy
        3. Promotional activities

III. PERFORMANCE

        1. Long-run cost-price differentials
        2. Industry progressivity

If these variables can be specified then we can predict the effect of changes in them upon competition.

The effects of a change in industry structure may take some time to work themselves out. Often, it is years after a structural change has occurred before meaningful performance data can be developed. If a change in the basic structure of an industry occurs as a result of the merger of two important firms, the effect is often immediate. We do not wait to observe the effect upon performance because we have strong reason to believe that competition will be harmed. We have an additional reason, however, to urge prompt action. Once the assets, personnel, and know-how of the two firms have been commingled, it is often impossible to separate the companies in a way which will reestablish the level of competition which had existed in the market. Consequently, some types of conduct, such as overt collusion as to price and market sharing, have become illegal *per se,* and some changes in structure, like horizontal acquisitions, have achieved a similar status. In these cases, experience has demonstrated that certain types of conduct and changes in industry structure inevitably yield adverse industry performance. As a consequence, economists tend to place considerable emphasis on the structure and conduct of industries.

ECONOMIC AND POLITICAL BACKGROUND

Our present concern with the adequacy of competitive conditions in individual markets and in the economy as a whole has its origin in many diverse areas. The passage of the Sherman Act (1890) marked the first formal legislative action in the U.S. recognizing the desirability of eliminating or prohibiting the further development of monopolistic power. Our concern with the nature of industry competition has both expanded and changed. At the present time, interest revolves around a number of specific questions. How well do industries in the economy perform? How is this performance measured? How serious are the actual deviations from the competitive norm? While our concern over deviations from competiton has increased since 1890, competition has declined markedly since then. We know of no causal relationship.

An objective analysis of the structure, conduct, and performance of markets of necessity requires the existence of some standard against which observed market conditions can be compared. The only body of economic thought available to us is that contained in the competitive economic model. This, of course, need not be the only method used. Standards of the behavior and performance of markets might be based upon a variety of other factors, both social and political. Those charged with public policy in this area often put social values above economic efficiency. For example, Congress has passed such economic and political monstrosities as the so-called "fair trade" laws and the Robinson-Patman Act. Both of these pieces of legislation were designed to circumvent economic efficiency and to encourage the needless continuation of small, often uneconomic-sized firms. For the most part, the effect has been minimal and the laws have failed to check the major abuses which are responsible for our major problems. This conclusion is based upon an analysis of the extent to which the apparent goals of the statutes are consistent with our usual standards of desirable economic performance. In passing, it contains an implicit answer to an unasked question: Do these specific laws aid in the efficient allocation of resources? The answer is, No!

On *a priori* grounds, it is generally considered that competitive markets provide the most economically desirable results. Let us look briefly at the conditions which exist and the results obtained in competitive markets. Again, they provide a simple model that can be used to trace the interrelationships which may exist between our three basic sets of competitive factors.

Structure: Many buyers and sellers, undifferentiated product, ease of entry and exit.

Conduct: Price, output, and product development decisions arrived at by the individual firm.

Performance: Long-run, price-cost differentials approach zero, long-run excess capacity is nonexistent, the scale of plant approaches optimum.

Judged in terms of the final results obtained in the market place (performance) this would clearly seem to provide the most economically efficient organization of industry. Significant departures from market structures that provide these desirable end results should be examined with considerable care.

What type of *conduct* and *performance* might one expect as the structure of the market is changed and passed through the entire spectrum from competition to monopoly? There are no simple and accurate answers to this question but we do have a number of *a priori* predictions that can be made. First, as the number of firms becomes smaller, firms must become aware of the fact that their individual actions have a measurable effect on the sales and profits of their competitors in the market. The reverse is true also. If they reduce prices, change products, and the like, they must expect their competitors to take countermeasures. In other words, the simple reduction in the number of firms results in the development of a variety of ways in which the sales strategy of individual firms tends to become limited. If this occurs in a competitive market, the response is an increase in general pressure for a reduction in market price. In competitive markets it is not possible to attach the blame for this to an individual firm. Consequently, no single firm bears the burden of reducing prices. In imperfectly competitive markets, however, the firms' responses may become somewhat more varied in a similar situation. A direct reduction of price, made with the hope of increasing sales, could well have an immediate and noticeable impact on other firms in the industry. It might bring about retaliatory price cuts by others with the result that the profits of all firms, including the price reduction initiator, would be reduced.

The firms placed in this situation would seem to be faced with a considerable problem. How does a firm increase its sales, while avoiding a form of behavior which is likely to be considered a direct attack on competitors? The firm may try to develop a strategy that induces buyers to purchase its product rather than those of its competitors because they get something in addition to what is available elsewhere. You have seen by this time that we have begun to open up a maze of twists and turns that characterizes interfirm behavior in imperfectly competitive industries. When is an attack not an attack? If price competition is not a real alternative, what is? One answer, of course, is product promotion. It should be emphasized, however, that this option is available only where real or apparent differences can be developed in the product itself or in the conditions surrounding the sale of the product. If successful, they may result in higher prices for the firms actively engaged in product promotion without affecting the price charged by others. Clearly they have raised cost. Such efforts have proved to be largely a waste of time when sellers are dealing with large, well-informed industrial or governmental buyers. Consequently, selling activities in such markets emphasize precise specifications, service, and corporate integrity. They are not usually accompanied by advertising campaigns involving large promotional expenditures.

The foregoing brief discussion is aimed at pointing up some major departures from competitive conduct which are found in imperfectly competitive industries. Of prime importance is the fact that firms lose (perhaps we should say that they gladly give up) some of the independence of action they have in competitive markets. An important problem centers about the economic consequences of this loss of independence. If the number of firms remaining in the market remains relatively large, its competitive significance may be slight. However, a substantial reduction in the number of firms may make some form of collusion, either tacit or overt, likely. Such agreements may range all the way from some form of "accepted" industry code of behavior at one extreme, to direct and detailed contacts between firms regarding prices, the sharing of markets and the like at the other extreme. If some complete form of collusion develops, then it may alter the basic *independent* profit maximization goals of the firms and consequently, the allocative efficiency of the market.

Avoidance of direct competitive responses introduces varieties of non-price competition; advertising is the most obvious of these, but they may include an intensification of efforts to improve or differentiate products, expand investment in basic research, and other means. Irrespective of the form of nonprice competition adopted, it is obvious that the immediate effect of these activities is higher costs. In the case of advertising, these are costs which the firm now makes to persuade buyers of the superiority of their product. The return may more than offset the costs incurred.

We have suggested only a few of the possible departures from the conduct which might be expected subsequent to a change in one basic structural condition, a reduction in the number of firms. Similar changes in conduct might be expected if entry conditions are altered. It is obvious that substantial possibilities exist for changes in the performance of industries as a result of structural changes *and* changes in conduct. However, it is not enough to know that changes in the basic structure and conduct of an industry will result in variations in performance. What kind of changes take place? How large are the performance changes in relation to the structural and conduct changes? Which changes in structure bring about the largest alterations in industry performance? Are the changes proportional, direct, measurable, significant, and so on?

Thus, the whole field of industrial organization analysis is built upon traditional economic theory, and could not exist without it. It goes somewhat further, however, and attempts to provide precise answers to questions of the type raised above. In this way, policy decisions with respect to the operation of our economy may be based upon precise knowledge rather than vague generalizations, and upon known relationships rather than articles of faith.

THE TECHNOLOGICAL BACKGROUND

Without doubt, one of the most, if not *the* most, important determinants of the evolving shape of our economy has been the rapid technological progress of the past century. In the past 100 years, we have witnessed an industrial transformation, both in terms of product and process, which is unparalleled in the history of man. Products of uniformly high quality are manufactured in completely automated plants at comparatively low costs. In many industries, rates of production have been accelerated through the introduction of large, capital-intensive equipment which obviates the necessity of a large number of small plants, producing essentially the same product. It has changed not only the way that we live, but the methods by which we produce those goods and services which sustain life. As a consequence of these developments, basic structural changes have occurred in major industries. In some cases, however, changes have occurred which have reduced the number of firms engaged in the industry, as well as increased the height of the barriers facing firms contemplating entry into such industries. Developments of the first type, where the result has been increased output and lowered costs of production and prices, are desirable and necessary to the progress of society.[4]

It does not follow that all reductions in the number of firms, with consequent increases in the size of those which remain, are the result of technological progress, nor that they result in expanded output and lowered costs. Herein lies the source of considerable confusion and controversy, some real, some contrived. Critics of antitrust policy regularly suggest that those agencies are insensitive to the technological changes that have occurred, and that as a result, they follow policies which retard rather than promote economic progress. The primary target for such thrusts is the reemphasis on the enforcement of Section 7 of the Clayton Act, as amended, which forbids certain types of mergers which may have the probable effect of reducing competition. A careful examination of the antimerger cases that have been filed since 1950 does not lend much support to the position that those agencies have failed to take into account technological changes which have resulted in greater efficiencies. Greater attention will be given in Chapters 2 and 3 to empirical evidence linking plant and firm size to efficiency.

The basic fact to be learned from the interaction of these changes upon the standards obtained from economic theory is that the norms of competitive theory must be modified in line with technological developments which affect efficiency. The evidence suggests that a good argument can be made in support of the position that technological progress, or the lack of technological progress, might be the most significant factor acting to reduce or inhibit competition. The argument has to be adapted to fit individual market conditions. Industries which have not experienced increases in technical innovation have tended to wither. The output of these industries has declined or, at best, remained steady. Costs have tended to rise and the number of firms in the industry has decreased with a consequent increase in concentration. On the other hand, some industries (those which have steady technical progress) have experienced just the reverse—new firms, rapid growth, lower costs, and declining concentration.

At the present time we can only imagine how the technical developments of the future will alter the form of our industrial structure.

[4] Edwin Mansfield, *The Economics of Technological Change*, W. W. Norton & Company Inc.: New York, 1968. This is one of the better new books on the subject containing systematic discussion of the patterns and problems of technological change from the point of view of the firm and society.

Symptomatic of the revolution under way is the IBM advertising slogan of mid-1968, "Men should think, machines should work." With the discovery of tremendous new energy sources, and the development of systems to harness and transform them into work, data retrieval systems will accomplish in a matter of minutes what now requires months of library research. Production processes will transform raw materials into finished products, without the use of millions of production workers. With all of these and other developments as yet unimagined, we may well arrive at the point where, for the first time in the history of mankind, we can transfer our energies to something more than a constant contest for physical survival.

We have not arrived at that state yet. Only the ignorant and the sanguine can really believe that we are experiencing a glut of goods and services. The level of living is quite high for many in our society. Despite this, many millions live at or below minimum acceptable levels of subsistence. Poverty is widespread, and the distance between the extremes in our society is not diminishing but expanding. The *Affluent Society* of Professor Galbraith is fiction not fact except for a subset of society in the United States and in the world.

Attention to efficiencies in the production process and to the elimination of conditions which impede the attainment of optimum efficiency are of vital importance. This alone will not accomplish the goal, but will represent a significant advance. We cannot afford to waste our scarce resources.

THE INDUSTRIAL SETTING

Employment Distribution   To a considerable degree the technical changes of the past 50 years have been reflected in the changing industrial makeup of our economy. A basic theme of our economic history, as well as that of other countries, has been a shift from an agrarian to an urban, nonagricultural society. Nowhere is the speed of that change more apparent than in an examination of shifts in employment that have occurred in the United States since 1950. In 1950, for example, 12 percent of our employed work force was engaged in some type of agricultural labor (see Table 1-1).

Since then, both the absolute number (and percentage) of agricultural workers has declined steadily. By 1970, the absolute number of farm workers was only 3.5 million (one-half the 1950 total). They accounted for only 4.5 percent of total noninstitutional employment. The simple fact is the United States is not heavily dependent upon agriculture for direct employment. As a matter of fact, only two other major industrial segments of the economy—mining and contract construction—are less important than agriculture as a source of employment (see Table 1-2).

Table 1-1   Non-institutional Employment by Major Division:
Selected Years 1950–1970[a]

YEAR	AGRICULTURE	ALL OTHERS	TOTAL CIVILIAN EMPLOYMENT
1950	7.2	51.8	58.9
1955	6.4	55.7	62.2
1960	5.5	60.3	65.8
1965	4.4	66.7	71.1
1970	3.5	75.2	78.6
Change	−51%	+45%	+33%

[a] Millions of persons 16 years of age and older.
Source: *Economic Report of the President*, February 1971, p. 222.

Where have the shifts occurred? Have all other segments grown relatively at the expense of agriculture, or has the growth been centered in a limited area? The data contained in Table 1-2, which shows nonagricultural employment by major industry group for 1940 and 1970, suggest answers to these questions. The data show three major changes which have occurred since 1940. Substantial increases have occurred in the share of total employment accounted for by the government and service sectors. In 1940, these two areas accounted for about 24 percent of total employment. By 1970, this had increased to 35 percent. On the other hand, the relative importance of manufacturing declined slightly from 34 percent to 27 percent.

Table 1-2   Wage and Salary Employees in Non-Agricultural
Establishments: 1940 and 1970
(All Employees, in Millions of Persons)

INDUSTRY GROUP	1940		1970	
	NUMBER	PERCENT OF TOTAL	NUMBER	PERCENT OF TOTAL
Mining	.9	3	.6	1
Contract Construction	1.3	4	3.3	5
Manufacturing	11.0	34	19.4	27
Transportation Commun. and Public Utilities	3.0	9	4.5	6
Trade	6.8	21	14.9	21
Finance, Insurance and Real Estate	1.5	5	3.7	5
Service and Miscellaneous	3.7	11	11.6	17
Government	4.2	13	12.6	18
TOTAL	32.4	100	70.7	100

Source: *Economic Report of the President*, February 1971, p. 228.

An examination of some of the intervening years shows that the bulk of decline in manufacturing employment has occurred since 1950. Since the share of national income accounted for by manufacturing remained the same over the 1950–1970 period, it would appear that the technical revolution of the past 25 years has made inroads upon manufacturing employment.

Company-Size Distribution   Over the past 25 years substantial changes have occurred in the number of companies in our economy. In 1939, there were approximately 1.8 million business units engaged in all types of business: about 75 percent of these firms were unincorporated businesses. By 1967, the number of businesses had increased to about 11.5 million; unincorporated businesses accounted for almost 90 percent of the total (Table 1-3).

Table 1-3   Number and Size of Business Units, by Type of Legal Organization: 1939, 1953, and 1967

Item		1939	1953	1967
Number[a]	Corporations	470	698	1,534
	Proprietorships and Partnerships	1,323	8,674	10,032
Receipts[b]	Corporations	$132.9	$558.2	$1,374.6
	Proprietorships and Partnerships	$ 38.3	$143.8	$ 289.4
Average Size[c]	Corporations	$282.8	$799.7	$ 896.1
	Proprietorships and Partnerships	$ 28.9	$ 16.5	$ 28.9

[a] Thousands of business units.
[b] Billions of Dollars.
[c] Business receipts per business unit in thousands of dollars.
Source: Internal Revenue Service, *Statistics of Income, Business Income Tax Returns,* various issues.

Despite the fact that the number of unincorporated businesses increased by almost 800 percent, their share of total business receipts declined slightly—from 22.4 percent to 17.4 percent. Also, the average size of unincorporated firms showed a decline in 1953 but rose again in 1967.

Throughout this period, corporations continued to grow in importance and in size. Average business receipts per corporate business tripled between 1939 and 1967. This shows only a part of the story. Equally interesting is the distribution of these corporations by asset-size class. Despite the fact that we tend to think of corporations as quite large, almost 91 percent of them have assets of $1 million or less. These, however, account for only about 10 percent of all corporate assets. On the other hand, corporations with assets of $1 billion or more hold almost one-half of the corporate assets.

Manufacturing Companies Only three major industrial divisions have any appreciable number of large corporations—finance and insurance, public utilities and manufacturing. The first two of these are under the direct control of specific State and Federal regulatory agencies. In effect we have admitted that competition does not exist in those industries. This may have occurred for a variety of reasons—some technical, some related to the simple politics of power, but most to the lack of interest on the part of the Congress, state legislatures and other governmental groups in maintaining competition. As a consequence, manufacturing remains the largest segment of our economy which is both inhabited by giant enterprises and subject to competitive pressures.

In 1970, there were approximately 193,000 incorporated and more than 213,000 unincorporated manufacturing companies. This number has grown steadily in recent years. Considerable disparities exist between number of firms and their economic power (Table 1-4). In manufacturing, corporations are substantially more important than in most other major industry divisions. It has been estimated that more than 98 percent of all manufacturing assets are held by corporate enterprises.[5] The corporate share has grown steadily since 1940.

Table 1-4 Distribution of Assets of Manufacturing Corporations, by Asset-Size Class: 1970

ASSET-SIZE CLASS	NUMBER OF FIRMS	Assets DOLLARS[a]	PERCENT
$1 Billion & over	102	267.7	48
$250 M–999.9 M	218	106.7	19
$100 M–249.9 M	289	45.1	8
$50 M–99.9 M	366	26.0	5
$25 M–49.9 M	533	19.1	3
$10 M–24.9 M	1,202	20.0	4
Under $10 M	190,000[b]	69.3	12

[a] Billions of dollars.
[b] Estimated.
Source: FTC-SEC, *Quarterly Financial Report for Manufacturing Corporations; First Quarter, 1970*, p. 61.

Not only does most of the economic power in the manufacturing segment reside in the hands of incorporated firms, it rests in the hands of a very few large corporations. In 1970, 102 companies accounted for 48 percent of all manufacturing assets. The largest 609 accounted for

[5] W. F. Mueller, "Statement," *Economic Concentration, Part 5—Overall and Conglomerate Aspects*, Hearings before the Senate Subcommittee on Antitrust and Monopoly, July, 1964, p. 114.

three-fourths of all corporate manufacturing assets. In total, this group of firms is equal to about .2 of 1 percent of all manufacturing corporations and less than .1 of 1 percent of all manufacturing firms.

There were 2,710 "large" corporations engaged in manufacturing (firms with assets of $10 million or more), or slightly more than one percent of all manufacturing corporations. This relatively small handful of firms accounts for more than 85 percent of the assets, sales and profits of all manufacturing companies, corporate and noncorporate. These figures suggest that economic power is closely held among a relatively small number of large manufacturing corporations. The competitive significance of this information has yet to be examined in meaningful market areas. It is sufficient at this point to note its existence.

SUMMARY

The purpose of this chapter has been to acquaint the reader with the study of industrial organization, its major elements (including a short descriptive glossary of terms to be used), and the relevance of the subject matter to traditional microeconomic theory. Brief mention was also made of the importance of technological change and its impact upon the rapidly changing structure of American industry.

The study of the detailed structure, conduct, and performance of American industry is sterile in the absence of some larger frame of reference. In this area, some attention has been devoted to the rapid change, even in recent years, in the agricultural-nonagricultural balance of our economy. Currently, one-third of our national income originates in manufacturing and it accounts for an equal share of total employment. Although its relative importance has declined slightly in the past 25 years, it remains by far the largest segment of economic activity.

Manufacturing is the only segment of our economy dominated by large firms where primary reliance is still upon the operation of the market economy. In other major industrial divisions where large firms dominate (banking, transportation, communication, public utilities, insurance and the like), the government has substituted nonmarket for market criteria in almost all important decision-making areas (prices, products, investment, service and the like). The results of almost all of these direct regulatory efforts have ranged from poor to terrible. If one had no other goal in a careful study of the structure, conduct and performance of American industry than to avoid repeating the faults of such actions, this would be enough.

APPENDIX TO CHAPTER 1:
MAJOR SOURCES OF
COMPANY AND INDUSTRY DATA

Those who are faced for the first time with the necessity of obtaining detailed economic data relating to the operation of firms and/or industries often find themselves at a loss. Unlike data relating to the overall operation of the economy, the sources of microeconomic data are varied. This brief guide to data sources is designed to provide the newcomer to research in this area with a starting place; it is not intended to be a complete or definitive catalog. Depending upon the student's research problem, interests and energy, the sources listed should suggest further research activity.

Individual Firm Data

Data related to the operation of individual companies and to their position in a given industry or product market are by far the most difficult to obtain. Many published sources present data which are typically too gross to provide the type of detail necessary for meaningful analysis. As a result, it is often necessary to use a variety of sources which pieced together may provide a fairly complete picture of a firm's economic activity. The best public sources include:

1. *Moodys' Industrial Manual.* These volumes are issued annually and contain historical and current financial data relating to all publicly-held manufacturing and other corporations and many closely-held (non-public) companies as well. Usually they contain a brief history of the

19

corporation, its major divisions, the locations of its plants, its domestic and foreign subsidiaries and affiliates and some information relating to minority interests in other corporations. In some instances it provides limited information relating to its products. It is one of the better public sources of data relating to a firm's past merger activity.

2. *Standard Corporation Record.* These reports are published annually and contain similar, though somewhat less complete, data to that contained in *Moodys'.* This does provide a good source from which to cross check data shown elsewhere.

3. *Standard and Poors' Industry Reports.* Brief surveys of a limited number of industries which show trends in industry growth and the identity and relative importance of the major companies in the industry.

4. *The Fortune Directory.* This *Report,* issued annually since 1955, contains sales, asset and profit data for the 500 largest listed industrial manufacturing corporations. The *Report* ranks firms by size of assets and sales. It does not include unlisted companies which becomes a serious omission for firms ranked between 200 and 500 on the list. The lists through 1965 have been collected by the Senate Subcommittee on Antitrust and Monopoly and appear as *Economic Concentration, Part 5B* (1967).

5. *Fortune Plant and Product Directory.* This directory contains detailed but often incomplete information on product mix, plant location and employment for almost all major manufacturing corporations. It does not have information relating to the relative importance of each of the products within the company.

6. *News Front Directory of Manufacturing Firms.* Contains data similar to that published by *Fortune.* It has two major advantages over the *Fortune* data, however. It is considerably more extensive in coverage, including about 20,000 firms. Also, it attempts to classify firms by major industry as well as by size.

7. *Annual Reports.* The individual company annual reports and prospectuses filed with the SEC provide limited financial information about the company. On occasion, however, they provide useful insights to the competitive attitudes of the firm with respect to its short-run goals, its relations with other firms, and the development and introduction of new products.

8. *Miscellaneous.* Other useful sources include reports in trade journals and trade papers, special reports by brokerage houses, *Thomas's Register,* Dun & Bradstreet directories and transcripts of proceedings before and decisions by regulatory agencies and courts. Antitrust proceedings, particularly those in which defendants are alleged to have adversely affected competition, are often of particular interest and value. Transcripts of hearings held before Federal regulatory commissions are

available in Washington, D.C.; those held before Federal district courts
are available in the city in which the trial is held.

Industry and Product Data

Industry data are available more readily than are company data.
However, in many cases the researcher will find that the product or industry classifications used are too gross to be of substantial analytical
value. He will find, however, that the more detailed the data, the less
often they are published and the longer will be the interval between the
collection of the data and their actual publication. The "best" sources
for product and industry data are usually reports by government agencies. The following agencies are prime sources of such data.

1. *U.S. Bureau of the Census.* These reports include the quinquennial
*Census of Manufacturers, Trade, Services, Mineral Industries, Agricul-
ture* and in 1963 a *Census of Transportation.* In manufacturing, for example, these reports show employment, number of companies and establishments, sales or shipments, value added, a limited number of cost
items, payroll and related data for all major (four-digit) industry and
most lesser (five- and seven-digit) product classifications. These reports
contain some state and Standard Metropolitan Statistical Area (SMSA)
data, as well as that for the entire country. In addition, the Bureau publishes an *Annual Survey of Manufactures* containing similar but less detailed industry and product class data. Frequent and often irreconcila-
ble changes in definition limit the usefulness of these data for historical
study.

2. *Internal Revenue Service.* Their published *Statistics of Income* series provides detailed industry sales, cost and profit data not available
elsewhere. The industry financial data shown are more detailed than
those which appear in any other source. Moreover, the presentation of
these data by asset-size class of firms makes it possible to conduct detailed intra-industry analysis by size of firm. These published data have
at least one major shortcoming—the industry classification is on a two-
digit basis. Unpublished data (the *Source Book*) are available on a
three-digit basis. The Internal Revenue Service data usually have a publication lag of from three to four years. Starting with the *1958 Census of
Manufactures,* the Bureau of the Census and the Internal Revenue Service began a "link" program for manufacturing industries. Among other
things it attempts to provide some of the IRS type data for Census categories. These data are usually restricted to three-digit industry group industry classifications.

3. *Federal Trade Commission.* The FTC, with the assistance of the
Securities and Exchange Commission, publishes the *Quarterly Financial*

Report for Manufacturing Corporations. This *Report*, which usually appears within three months of the close of each quarter, provides limited income and balance sheet data for manufacturing corporations by two-digit industry group and by asset-size classes. The *Report* contains substantially less detail than do the IRS Reports but it provides more current data than any similar report.

Since 1914, the Federal Trade Commission has published a series of more than 100 monographs dealing with the competitive behavior of individual firms and industries, and with the competitive effects various types of behavior. These studies often prove useful as a point of departure for additional research activity. While the FTC merger series which now appears as *Current Trends in Merger Activity* is the best which is available publicly, even this series is quite deficient.

4. *The Business and Defense Services Administration (BDSA).* This agency's published reports provide substantial information regarding a wide range of industries and products. Most of these reports are regular monthly publications which usually contain detailed output and occasionally some price data. They include, in many cases, selected cost and shipment data which are keyed to the appropriate *Census of Manufactures* classifications. These data are typically collected from secondary sources.

5. *Bureau of Old Age and Survivors Insurance.* In cooperation with the Bureau of the Census, this part of the Department of Health, Education and Welfare (HEW) publishes annually the *County Business Patterns.* These reports show the number and employment size of manufacturing and other establishments on a county, state and national level. These data are presented on a four-digit industry classification basis. Typically, they include all establishments which employ three or more employees. These reports are based on similar information which is collected by individual State Departments of Employment Security.

6. *Other Important Governmental Sources.* Four other agencies publish some industry and product information (limited to a narrow range of industries): (*a*) The *Department of Agriculture* publishes considerable data related to raw materials and some processed agricultural products (agriculture extension departments of State Universities may be useful in this area). These data include detailed output, cost and farm income data on a county and state basis. (*b*) The *U. S. Tariff Commission* regularly publishes detailed import and export product data, as well as a variety of special reports on products which may be affected by imports. These reports are particularly useful in research involving the production of inorganic chemicals. (*c*) The *Bureau of Mines* publishes a variety of reports which estimate the demand, production and inventory characteristics of various mineral products. (*d*) The *Bureau of Labor Statistics* (BLS) publishes the most complete and detailed wholesale and retail

price data available. Since these data are based upon published or list prices, they well may underestimate the magnitude of actual price declines in "soft" markets. In such periods, there is a general tendency for firms to engage in considerable "off-list" selling. The less competitive industries become, the more likely it is that this form of behavior occurs.

If your research goes into regulated areas, considerable data are available from state and Federal regulatory agencies.

7. *Congressional Sources.* Useful economic information relating to industry behavior has been published from time to time by the Joint Economic Committee, the House and Senate Committees on Small Business, and the House and Senate Subcommittees on Antitrust and Monopoly. The Senate Subcommittee on Antitrust and Monopoly is perhaps the most active in this area with its *Concentration Ratios in Manufacturing Industry* (1954, 1958, and 1963) and its *Hearings on Economic Concentration* (1964 through 1967). This set of Hearings contains some of the more recent and most useful data which have been collected and used for the study of industrial organization problems in the past 25 years.

Special commissions and committees occasionally publish usable economic data. Two notable instances are (*a*) the *Temporary National Economic Committee* (TNEC), which published more than 40 monographs of interests to students of this area in the period immediately prior to World War II, and (*b*) the *National Commission on Food Marketing,* which in 1966 published a rather interesting set of technical reports dealing with various phases of food processing and distribution.

8. *Private Sources.* There is virtually no end to the number of private sources of industry and product data. Unfortunately, these data are fragmentary and incomplete and are usually gathered by groups not primarily interested in shedding light on the competitive conduct and performance of industries. In addition to the private sources of data mentioned above, the researcher might examine the publication lists of the National Industrial Conference Board, the National Bureau of Economic Research and the Committee on Economic Development. Finally, every major trade association has a research department which collects economic data. Some of these data are published.

That is a start; from here you follow the yellow brick road.

2

THE STRUCTURE OF AMERICAN INDUSTRY: I

This is the first of two chapters which concentrate on the identification and measurement of some of the major factors which determine the structure of American industry. Unless we examine these vital factors in detail we cannot realize the basic importance of industry structure to all forms of conduct and performance. While it is not possible to predict the *precise* form that these will take as the result of a given set of structural factors, it is clear that certain combinations of structural characteristics will lead to predictable types of conduct and performance.

We are fortunate to have substantial quantities of economic data relating to the structure of industry. Much of it is general; other data, however, are very specific. These data are useful in appraising competitive conditions in individual industries, and in the production of specified products and product classes. This chapter is devoted to the study of economic concentration—its measurement, recent trends in broad industry segments and individual industries, and the major factors which appear to be responsible for changes in the level of concentration. The chapter ends with a discussion of the importance of merger activity as a contributing factor to recent changes in the level of concentration in the manufacturing and trade areas. Chapter 3 will deal with questions of the importance of product differentiation, the economic significance of barriers to entry, and some related problems.

CONCENTRATION DEFINED

The terms "economic concentration," "business concentration," and "market concentration" are among the more overused terms employed in the study of industrial organization. The reason for this is quite simple. It is the single most important characteristic which describes the level or extent of competition in some segments of the economy. In its simplest form it represents no more than a shorthand method of describing the extent to which *n* number of firms control *x* percent of the sales, productive capacity, profits, assets or some other variable of a given market area. In dealing with specific industry and product concentration, it is usual to look at the share held (controlled) by the four largest firms.[1] In measuring the extent of concentration in larger segments, such as all manufacturing, the shares of a larger number of firms are usually presented, for instance the 20, 50, 100, or 200 largest firms. The specific measure used depends, in large part, on the goals of the study in question, and the availability of meaningful data.

Measures of concentration are rough indications of the relative size distribution of firms in some given population. They are an objective measure of the control of some selected economic variable. Nothing more! By themselves, they have no normative connotation. Before a concentration ratio can take on competitive significance, that is, before it can be used in some normative sense, it must be related to a particular industrial situation. An eight-firm concentration ratio of 20 percent is obviously low, but it is not necessarily good. On the other hand, a concentration ratio of 50 percent is generally considered to be *high* but on *a priori* grounds alone it is not necessarily *bad*.

It is true that, other things being equal, the larger the degree of control exercised by the leading firms (the higher the level of concentration) the less likely it will be that the conduct and performance typically associated with competitive markets will prevail. The actual competitive results depend upon the number and relative size of firms, industry growth and other factors that will be examined later in this chapter. In an area so fraught with feelings regarding the "good guys" and the "bad guys," it is easy to be overcome by a form of emotional confusion between high and low on the one hand, and bad and good on the other. Such confusion is inexcusable for an economist.

---

[1] Data are available which show 8, 20, and 50 firm concentration ratios for all manufacturing industries in 1947, 1954, 1958, 1963, 1966, and 1967 in: U.S. Bureau of the Census, Census of Manufactures, 1967, *Special Report Series: Concentration Ratios in Manufacturing*, MC 67(S) 2.1, Part 1. Pp. SR-2, 3.

MEASURES OF CONCENTRATION

The use of concentration ratios in economic analysis implies that the user has an understanding of three basic and highly interrelated problems: their development, use, and interpretation. These may be best examined by providing answers to three questions. First, what is being measured? Second, how is it being measured? [2] Finally, for what segment of the economy is concentration being measured? Hopefully the answers to these questions will provide some light in this rather murky area.

Selection of Variables   Studies of concentration have been prepared using many different variables. Most questions regarding the selection of variables have been decided on one of two grounds. What do you want to measure? What is available which may be used to provide the desired information? Since most studies of concentration are devoted to an examination of the extent to which a small group of firms has "economic power," general financial and output variables have been used. The major exceptions are those studies which have tried to measure technical advantage. Studies of the impact of defense expenditures on competition have looked at both the distribution of research and development expenditures, and awards of Federal government contracts. Some studies of this area have looked at the distribution of patent grants. This latter type of study might best be examined along with general questions relating to entry barriers.

The most popular variables which have been selected are value of shipments, value added, net capital assets (plant and equipment value less depreciation) and total assets. The first two have been used primarily in studies of 4-digit industry and 5-digit product class concentration because of their availability from *Census of Manufactures* data. Like other census data, these are not available on a company basis but are collected for plants producing items which can be classified into industries as product classes.

Total and net capital assets have the advantage that they provide a relatively good indication of the productive strength of a whole company, as well as its overall financial capabilities. In this sense, the total asset measure is probably the better of the two. The net capital asset figure is probably a better measure of the vertical integration of firms. The measurement of asset concentration has been used in dealing with broad industry sectors which typically include an entire company's op-

---

[2] This is a highly technical question and will not be dealt with at this point. Should the reader be interested in additional study, he should read: Gideon Rosenbluth, "Measures of Concentration," *Business Concentration and Price Policy*, NBER (Princeton), 1955, pp. 57–95; also O. C. Herfindahl, "Comment," *Ibid.*, pp. 95–100.

eration. Therefore, such data are not generally available on a 4-digit industry basis. It is not possible at the present time to obtain detailed data that separate a multiproduct corporation's assets along narrow industry or product lines.

A little-used, but extremely interesting variable for the measurement of concentration is net income of the leading corporations. This variable is perhaps the best of the measures of the current financial strength of a business. It is a clear indication of the firm's present power. Data availability limits its use since profit figures *per se* are not collected by the Bureau of the Census.

Is there any *general* relationship among the results obtained using these major variables? One recent study of industry concentration uses all of these major variables in a single analysis with interesting results.[3] The results of that study suggest that there is a general relationship between the relative level of concentration and the particular variable that is used.

The study looks at the 4-firm and 20-firm concentration ratios for 28 2- and 3-digit industry groups, as measured by sales, assets, net capital assets and net income after taxes.[4] Table 2-1 summarizes those data, and ranks each of the variables on the basis of the number of times the concentration ratio for each variable was the highest, second, third or lowest in those industry groups.

Table 2-1   Relationship Between the Importance of Four Variables as Measures of Concentration in 28 Selected Industry Groups: Fourth Quarter, 1962 (number of times each variable appears in each rank)

Rank	Sales	Total Assets	Net Capital Assets	Income After Taxes
Highest	1	1	10	16
Second	1	15	8	4
Third	4	10	6	8
Lowest	22	2	4	0

Source: W. F. Mueller, "Statement," *Economic Concentration, Part 1—Overall and Conglomerate Aspects,* Hearings before Senate Subcommittee on Antitrust and Monopoly, July 2, 1964, pp. 117–120.

The results show that: (1) concentration measures based upon sales data appear to be the lowest; (2) total assets are seldom highest or low-

[3] W. F. Mueller, "Statement," *Economic Concentration, Part 1—Overall and Conglomerate Aspects,* Hearings before the Senate Subcommittee on Antitrust and Monopoly, July 2, 1964, pp. 109–129.
[4] *Ibid.,* pp. 117–120.

est; (3) net capital assets generally show higher concentration ratios than either sales or total assets; and (4) on the average, net income after taxes (profits) gives the highest level of concentration. Depending upon the desires of the researcher to obtain a "high" or a "low" concentration ratio, he can assist his cause by the "proper" selection of the variable to be used. If one is interested in measuring economic power, then he is advised to select those variables which are the best indicators of such strength. Assets and net income would seem the best to be used in such cases, the first as an indicator of potential economic power, and the latter as a manifestation of actual strength in the market place.

Type of Concentration   Economic power may be measured in a variety of settings. It is incumbent upon the researcher to select an industry setting consistent with the purpose of the study. In dealing with a study of the relative concentration of power it may be most relevant to select a group of firms producing a single product, or a group of similar products, in a limited geographic area. In other cases, it may be appropriate to select a similar product definition but a somewhat larger market area. In both cases, however, the area of competition is limited by the product. As a consequence, concentration measures of this type are generally referred to as *specific* measures of concentration. They measure the relative size of leading firms in narrowly defined areas of competition. As long as the actual area of competition between firms is confined to narrow product or industry lines, such measures of concentration are appropriate and adequate.

The rapid rise in the importance of conglomerate firms suggests that the measurement of actual areas of competition between major firms in the economy may require a broader market definition. The expansion of firms into new, but related, areas of activity *via* merger (product-extension mergers) has been the subject of recent antitrust litigation.[5] In addition, studies have been made which show the extent to which large manufacturing firms have diversified into different industries in the post-war period.[6] Some studies are available which show the extent to which firms have diversified into a number of closely related products within broad 2-digit industry groups. A recent study of this type shows not only the extent of such diversification in food manufacturing, but the methods employed in achieving the existing diversification levels.[7]

Studies of this type look at the extent of concentration in a broader area: a single 2-digit industry group like *food and kindred products*, a

---

[5] *In the Matter of Procter & Gamble Company*, FTC Docket No. 6901, Opinion of The Commission.

[6] See, for example, Michael Gort, *Diversification and Integration in American Industry*, National Bureau of Economic Research, 1962, pp. 27–64, *passim*.

[7] FTC, *The Structure of Food Manufacturing, op. cit.*, p. 121–130.

broader one like *all manufacturing,* or *all non-financial corporations.* All such measures of concentration are referred to as *general* measures of concentration. As the area of competition between firms expands (as firms become more diversified), the 2-digit concentration measures may well shift from general to specific categories. Basically, however, the emphasis of such studies is upon the overall concentration of economic power.

The meaning and significance of specific concentration measures is relatively clear. Here the analysis is concerned with the extent to which economic control is exercised over the sale and manufacture of a particular product, or group of products, by a small number of firms. The possible adverse consequences of an increase in concentration are fairly clear. First, buyers of the product may be adversely affected (in the form of higher prices) by a reduction in active competition among firms as a result of increases in disparities in firm size. Second, existing small firms may find themselves at a disadvantage in dealing with their stronger and larger competitors. They may become reluctant to be too vigorous in their efforts to attract sales. Third, firms contemplating entry into a market may be deterred by the fact that a substantial portion of the market is in the hands of a few large, well-entrenched producers.

What do general measures of concentration show? What is the significance of the fact that the 20 largest manufacturing corporations held 25 percent of the assets of all manufacturing firms in the fourth quarter of 1962?[8] Is the presence of a high level of general concentration the equivalent of a low level of competition? The answers that have been developed by economists to these and related problems are not always clear.

High or rising levels of general concentration have been looked upon with substantial disfavor. This grows out of our general beliefs regarding the effectiveness of competition as a regulator of the flow of resources in economic activity. However, does an increase in the general level of concentration of decision making within the economy adversely affect the level and intensity of competition in individual markets? In the absence of any other information one might conclude that it is not overall concentration which determines the character and effectiveness of competition between firms. These are determined by the degree of concentration within each individual market. If all manufacturing firms were engaged in the production of the same products then the present concentration levels might not constitute any serious problem. The fact remains, however, that the output of these firms is classified into 20 major industry groups, into more than 400 4-digit industry groups and into more than 1,000 product classes. The high level of concentration in

[8] Mueller, *op. cit.,* p. 113.

the economy as a whole then reflects substantially higher levels of concentration in individual industries and product classes. Rising levels of concentration in the overall economy reflects a rise in concentration in individual industries. Moreover, rising levels of diversification suggest that classifications broader than the 4-digit industry are actually the areas of competition most relevant in appraising its vigor. Public interest in changes in the level of general concentration is desirable because the high and increasing levels of diversification which prevail in our economy make it the *relevant* area of interfirm relationship.[9]

A concentration ratio is basically a measure of the inequality of distribution of some variable, usually wealth, income or output. The existing level of inequality of wealth or income (as well as changes in it) has a substantial effect on the distribution of political power within the country. Given the basic democratic orientation of our political philosophy, it is not surprising that we tend to the belief that large centers of economic power, as well as centers of political power should be viewed with considerable suspicion. This is particularly true when direct control cannot be exercised over the holders of that power by the members of that society. We are concerned, therefore, with conditions which perpetuate or extend the span of control of a few firms or individuals.

Some question the effectiveness of the control which is alleged to exist in the hands of an advantaged few. Many contend, for example, that the current level of asset accumulation is no cause for alarm. They cite offsets which exist in the system, and which serve to dilute any such power. This view of our society does not command great support, nor does it seem to be borne out by either the economic or political "facts of life." Bain suggests, for example, that equating the distribution of wealth with a diminution of competitive force "shifts the argument from the power question *per se* to the analysis of competition and monopoly as related to market structures, and raises a distinct set of issues."[10] This approach to the problem ignores the fact that it is not and never has been a question of "size" *per se* which obtains the primary attention of economists, but "power," which is always relative and never absolute. Power is necessarily defined within some frame of reference. The more extended the scope of activities of firms, the broader must be the market within which the measurement occurs, and the more reduced is their power.

Both *specific* and *general* measures of concentration serve to expand the area of knowledge regarding the extent and strength of competition

[9] M. A. Adelman, "The Measurement of Industrial Concentration," *The Review of Economics and Statistics*, November 1951, p. 271.

[10] Joe S. Bain, *Industrial Organization*, 2nd ed., New York, John Wiley & Sons, Inc., 1968, p. 91.

in narrow and broad segments of the economy.[11] They should not be regarded as alternative methods of approaching the analysis of industrial organization problems, but as complementary; the knowledge gained in one area adds to and reinforces information obtained in others.

RECENT CHANGES IN CONCENTRATION

Attempts to measure the actual extent of economic concentration have been restricted to the past 50 years. Some general observations can be made regarding concentration in earlier periods, but at best, they must be treated as little more than informed guesses as to the general path of change. The basic reason for this is the inability to obtain accurate estimates of the wealth, income, sales or profits for broad segments of the economy during these early years. As yet, no analytical procedure has been developed which will overcome a lack of data.

Although no precise measures of concentration exist for the pre-1900 period, it appears that prior to about 1870, manufacturing industry was small (less than 30 percent of all national income) and apparently atomistic. Over the next 35 years, this situation changed considerably in two ways. First, concurrent with the improvement in sources of energy and means of transportation, manufacturing increased considerably in importance. Industry moved out of the woodshed and into the factory. Second, manufacturing industry became considerably more concentrated. The basic reason for this change was probably the great wave of merger activity which swept the country between 1880 and 1905. In his *Truth About Trusts* (1905), John Moody estimated that more than 5,000 independent manufacturing plants disappeared by merger between 1880 and 1904. The 300 or more companies which evolved controlled some 40 percent of all capital invested in manufacturing activities in this country.[12] Moody's estimates do little more than indicate that: (1) concentration in manufacturing industry had grown substantially prior to 1905; (2) merger activity was probably the basic cause of the growth; and (3) little was known about the extent of concentration in areas outside manufacturing.

[11] It is interesting and not coincidental that societies which place considerable reliance upon the widespread participation of the population in the democratic processes, also place considerable reliance upon free and competitive markets for the most efficient allocation of goods and services. Societies which have a long tradition of central control seem undisturbed by the centralization of economic power. As would be expected, they do place stress upon the registration of such combines, and insist that the governing body be well-informed regarding their actions.

[12] John Moody, *The Truth About Trusts*, Westport, Conn., Greenewood Press, Inc., 1905.

Broad Sector Concentration Studies

Most contemporary studies of industrial concentration use 1929 as a starting point. This is really an accident of economic history, growing out of the general economic collapse which began in October of that year, for which the blame was often put upon business, and the availability of the first sets of reliable statistics for manufacturing firms. The "great depression" was responsible for volumes of studies which purported to examine the basic structure of our economy, and the causes for its failure. The most important of these was the epoch study by Gardiner Means and Adolph Berle, *The Modern Corporation and Private Property*. Based upon data which first became available in 1931, Means began the first systematic study of economic concentration.

The first studies in this area dealt with the "nonfinancial" corporate sector of the economy. A later study which Means directed suggested that the 200 largest nonfinancial corporations accounted for 47.9 percent of the assets of all nonfinancial corporations in 1929.[13] This group accounted for about 58 percent of all capital assets. Between 1929 and 1933, the downturn of the depression, concentration appears to have increased considerably. Assets held by the 200 largest corporations increased from 47.9 percent to 54.9 percent. Those held by the 75 largest manufacturing corporations increased from 36.2 percent to 40.2 percent.

In their first study, Berle and Means had predicted that if the growth rate of the 200 largest corporations between 1924 and 1929 was maintained until 1950, this group would hold 85 percent of all corporate wealth.[14] The changes which occurred between 1929 and 1933 would not lead one to revise this estimate. Fortunately, the direction of this movement changed during the remainder of the prewar period.

Two rather good sets of estimates of the changes of concentration during the depression period exist. The first is contained in a study of the 1919–1958 period by Collins and Preston.[15] Their estimates are shown in Table 2-2.

The data presented below bears out in large part the pattern of concentration observed by Berle and Means in the pre-1929 period. It also shows that at least with respect to the 100 largest firms, concentration continued to increase through the early years of the depression. Unfortunately, their data for the years between 1935 and 1948 are not sufficiently detailed to make it possible to identify the timing of the changes that took place.

The Collins and Preston data indicate, however, that concentration showed a measurable increase in the post-World War II period. Be-

[13] *The Structure of the American Economy*, National Resources Committee, 1939.
[14] Berle and Means, *op. cit.*, p. 40.
[15] N. R. Collins and L. E. Preston, "The Size Structure of Industrial Firms," *The American Economic Review*, December 1961, pp. 986–1011.

tween 1948 and 1958, the share of assets held by the 100 largest corporations increased from 26.7 percent to 29.8 percent of all corporate assets. The increase in concentration over that period shown by their data underestimates, if anything, the magnitude of the change which has occurred. The bulk of the firms included in the analysis were manufacturing firms. However, the relative importance of unincorporated manufacturing companies has declined considerably over the past few decades. Census and IRS data indicate that unincorporated firms may have held as much as 20 percent of the value of all manufacturing assets in the period around 1919. By 1947, this figure had declined to about 6 percent [16] and by 1962 to less than 2 percent.[17] Thus, earlier figures of concentration (around 1919), which took only *corporations* into account, probably overestimated those values by as much as 10 to 15 percent.

Table 2-2   Asset Concentration of Mining, Manufacturing and Distribution Corporations by Size Group: 1919–1958

Size Group	Year				
	1919	1929	1935	1948	1958
4 largest	4.0	6.6	5.4	5.7	6.8
20 largest	8.3	15.0	13.1	14.0	16.1
100 largest	16.6[a]	25.5	28.0	26.7	29.8

[a] Estimated from Internal Revenue Service data on total population less subtractions in other than listed areas.
Source: N. R. Collins and L. E. Preston, "The Size Structure of Industrial Firms," *The American Economic Review*, December 1961, p. 989, Table 1.

Some of the recent studies of the post-World War II period avoid the obvious errors included in the Kaplan,[18] Adelman,[19] and Collins and Preston [20] data. Most of these analyses have appeared since 1964 in testimony before the Senate Sub-Committee on Antitrust and Monopoly, and the Senate Select Committee on Small Business. The first of these data sets appears in the testimony of John Blair, in the *Economic Concentration* hearings referred to earlier. Blair's data refer to concentration changes in value added by manufacture for the 200 largest manufacturing companies over the period 1947–1963. (Table 2-3)

These data, reflecting only changes in the manufacturing sector, show even more clearly the substantial increase in overall concentration

[16] FTC, *Report on the Concentration of Productive Facilities, 1947*, 1949, p. 16.
[17] Mueller, *op. cit.*, p. 121.
[18] A. D. H. Kaplan, *Big Enterprise in a Competitive System*, rev. ed., The Brookings Institution, 1964, p. 119ff.
[19] M. A. Adelman, *op. cit.*, pp. 285–290 *passim*.
[20] Collins and Preston, *op. cit.*

which has occurred since 1947. Between 1947 and 1967, for example, the share of total value added accounted for by the 50 largest manufacturing firms increased from one-sixth of the total to one-fourth—a relative increase of 50 percent. The increased dominance of the larger firms is seen from the fact that in 1967, the 100 largest accounted for one-third of all value added, while the 200 largest accounted for 42 percent of the total.[21] Given the fact that there were 401,014 manufacturing firms in 1967, the figure indicates a high and growing level of corporate control in the manufacturing sector.

Table 2-3   Concentration of Value Added by Manufacture by the 200 Largest Manufacturing Firms: 1947, 1954, 1963, and 1967

SIZE GROUP	Year			
	1947	1954	1963	1967
50 largest	17	23	25	25
100 largest	23	30	33	33
200 largest	30	37	41	42

Source: U.S. Bureau of the Census, Census of Manufactures, 1967, *Special Report Series: Concentration Ratios in Manufacturing*, MC 67(S)-2.1, Part I, Table 1.

One final set of data showing concentration changes in the manufacturing sector is presented in Table 2-4. These data show changes in the asset holdings of all manufacturing companies over the period 1925 to 1968. These data appear in *Economic Report on Corporate Mergers*, recently published by the Federal Trade Commission.

These data show quite clearly the changes which have occurred in overall concentration in the manufacturing sector over the past 44 years. In 1968, for example, the 100 largest firms held 48.8 percent of all manufacturing assets, more than the share which was held by the 200 largest held in 1929. The most rapid growth took place over the period between 1948 and 1958. The data show, however, that the already high levels attained by 1958 were not only maintained but increased slightly by 1968.

The statistical material referred to thus far indicates that regardless of the data set selected, the trend toward increased concentration is clear and unmistakable. Switching from one variable to another only serves to substantiate the earlier point that the selection of variable for use in the measurement of concentration changes the level, but not the direction or magnitude of the movement.

They indicate, also, that the conventional wisdom which suggests that high levels of concentration can be offset by rapid economic growth may not be the general case. This rather sanguine attitude was probably

[21] The data show that the bulk of the increase appeared to occur between 1947 and 1954.

Table 2-4   Share of Manufacturing Assets Held
by the 100 and 200 Largest Corporations:
1925–1941 and 1948–1968

	Share of 100 largest		Share of 200 largest	
YEAR	TOTAL ASSETS	CORP. ASSETS	TOTAL ASSETS	CORP. ASSETS
1925	34.5	36.1	—	—
1927	34.4	36.6	—	—
1929	38.2	39.7	45.8	47.7
1931	41.7	43.4	49.0	50.9
1933	42.5	44.2	49.5	51.4
1935	40.8	42.3	47.7	49.6
1937	42.1	43.7	49.1	50.9
1939	41.9	43.5	48.7	50.5
1941	38.2	39.6	45.1	46.7
1948	38.6	40.3	46.3	48.3
1950	38.4	39.8	46.1	47.7
1952	39.3	40.6	47.7	49.2
1954	41.9	43.3	50.4	52.1
1956	43.9	45.0	52.8	54.1
1958	46.0	47.1	55.2	56.6
1960	45.5	46.4	55.2	56.3
1962	45.5	46.2	55.1	56.0
1964	45.8	46.5	55.8	56.1
1966	45.8	46.4	56.1	56.7
1968	48.8	49.3	60.4	60.9

Source: FTC, *Economic Report on Corporate Mergers*, October 1969, p. 173.

encouraged by the fact that an increase in concentration occurred in the early years of the depression (1929–1933), but that it declined as business conditions improved up to 1941. While the recent experience is too short to draw any general conclusions regarding the relationship between economic growth and concentration (if one does in fact exist), it does suggest that those who advocate a permissive antitrust policy, in the conviction that efforts spent on increasing economic growth would improve levels of general welfare through an increase in both the quantity of goods and services available and a reduction in losses due to market imperfections, might seriously reexamine their conclusions.

Industry Concentration Studies

Industry concentration studies are considerably narrower in scope and depict the share of industry's sales which are accounted for by the most important firms in that industry. Industry concentration measures commonly used refer to the share of total industry shipments which are accounted for by the 4, 8 or 20 largest producers in that industry.[22] It is easy to place too great a reliance upon such a single-purpose measure. The user should be aware of the limitations of such a measure before going too far in using it as the sole measure of basic market structure, or as the distinguishing feature between the structures of between two or more industries.

Four examples from *Concentration Ratios in Manufacturing: 1967* illustrate the problems inherent in the use of any single measure. The problems in the use of a single measure of concentration are pointed up by answering the following question: Which of the following industries has the more (or less) competitive market structure?

	Industry Title			
CONCENTRATION LEVEL	DEHYDRATED FOODS	HATS AND CAPS	STEEL PIPES AND TUBES	ELECTRONIC COMPONENTS
4-Firm	32	32	32	32
8-Firm	50	41	45	38
20-Firm	75	58	72	51
50-Firm	96	71	92	65
Number of firms	134	340	123	1775

If only the 4-firm concentration is taken into account it would appear that an equal degree of concentration is present in all of the industries. A comparison of 8-firm ratios, however, indicates that industries *A* and *C* are somewhat more concentrated than are industries *B* and *D*. At the 20-firm level a substantial gap (24 percent) has been opened with the industries ranked in order of concentration—*A, C, D,* and *B*. At the 50-firm level, the spread is even greater—31 points—although the order remains the same. Do these figures portray accurately the relative competitive structure in these industries? Is concentration the lowest (or is the structure more competitive) in industry *D*? If the relative number of firms in industries *C* and *D* is taken into account, the answer is not as clear. This information is obtained by looking at the level of concentration for successive size classes of firms. The use of a single cumulative measure might simplify the inter-industry comparisons, as well as intra-industry changes through time. One form of summary measure is a simple sum of the squares approach based upon the marginal contribution of each size class to total concentration. If a single firm controlled an entire industry, the coefficient would be 1.0. The coefficients for the firms used in the example are .2193 (industry *A*), .1395 (industry

[22] The use of the terms largest and leading throughout this section refers to the importance of the firms in terms of their industry sales; not in terms of their total size or sales.

B), .2094 (industry *C*), and .1244 (industry *D*). On this basis, the summary figures yield results identical with those obtained by the first method. In a study to determine the "best" measure of concentration [23] Boyle and Bailey concluded that all standard measures of concentration give essentially the same results.

Table 2-5   Distribution of High Concentration Industries by Major Industry Group: 1967

| | *Industries* [a] | |
INDUSTRY GROUP	HIGH CONCENTRATION	ALL [b]
All industries	101	413
Food products	13	44
Tobacco manufactures	4	4
Textile products	8	29
Apparel and related products	1	33
Lumber and wood products	1	13
Furniture and fixtures	0	12
Paper and allied products	2	17
Printing and publishing	1	15
Chemicals and allied products	12	28
Petroleum and coal products	1	5
Rubber and plastic products	3	5
Leather and leather products	1	10
Stone, clay and glass	9	27
Primary metal industry	4	23
Fabricated metal products	5	29
Machinery, excluding electrical	8	38
Electrical machinery	16	33
Transportation equipment	7	15
Instruments and related products	3	11
Miscellaneous manufacturing	3	22

[a] "All" shows the number of 4-digit industries in each industry group. "High Concentration" shows the number of 4-digit industries in each industry group in which the 4-firm concentration ratio is 50 percent or higher.

[b] Shipment figures are in millions of dollars.

Source: Computed from *Concentration Ratios in Manufacturing Industry: 1963*, Part 2, Table 6, MC 69(S)–2.2.

A brief look at the present level of concentration in some of our more important large industries suggests the range of concentration in American industry. Table 2-5, for example, shows the distribution of the high concentration industries by major two-digit industry groups in 1967.

[23] Stanley E. Boyle and Duncan Bailey, "The Optimal Measure of Concentration," Paper presented at the meetings of the Western Economic Association, August 1970, *passim.*

These figures show that areas of high concentration tend to be bunched in certain industry groups. There is only one industry group in which there are no high concentration industries as they are defined here; five more in which there is only one highly concentrated industry; and an additional four in which there are two or three highly concentrated industries. In total, however, these ten industry groups accounted for less than 32 percent of all 413 industries included, and less than 30 percent of total employment and shipments. On the other hand, the eight industry groups which account for the bulk of the highly concentrated industries include about 60 percent of total manufacturing employment and shipments. Thus, high concentration would seem to be more prevalent in the larger, more important industry groups.

The relationship between size and concentration is many times overemphasized in these figures. The study of industrial organization is primarily concerned with the relationship between the structure of the industry and resulting conduct and performance. Consequently, relatively little attention is paid to the absolute size of industries as measured by shipments or some other variable. Such a measure would show only those areas of greatest economic significance. Rather, we are interested in those industries which, because of their present structure or recent changes in their structure, are or give some promise of becoming significant problem areas. One method of approaching this problem is to look at size and concentration at the same time (see Table 2-6).

Table 2-6   Distribution of Industries by Size of Value
of Shipments and 4-Firm Concentration Ratio: 1967

CONCENTRATION SIZE CLASS [a]	*Industry Shipments Size Class* [b]				
	ALL	OVER 1000	500–999	200–499	UNDER 200
Total [c]	413	134	91	100	67
80% and over	16	4	3	5	4
50% –79%	86	25	21	19	21
20% –49%	195	66	42	54	33
Under 20%	95	39	25	22	9
Insufficient data	21	—	—	—	—

[a] 4-firm ratio on basis of value of shipments.
[b] Shipments figures are in millions of dollars.
[c] Data only available for 413 or 417 industry classes.
Source: Computed from *Special Report Series: Concentration Ratios in Manufacturing*, Part 2, Table 6, MC 67(S)–2.2.

These data show that almost one-fourth of all industries have 4-firm concentration ratios of 50 percent or more. The reader should not assume that the problem of monopoly control is unimportant or nonexistent on the basis of these figures. Many economists interested in industrial organization suggest that the critical market share figure is 50 percent for the 8 largest firms in the industry.[24] Moreover, these measures ignore the fact that the relevant market area in many industries is local or regional, rather than nationwide. In many of these, the local area concentration figures are quite high despite low national figures.

Table 2-7   Selected Manufacturing Industries, by Value of Shipments
4- and 8-Firm Ratios: 1967

4-DIGIT INDUSTRY	4-FIRM RATIO	8-FIRM RATIO	VALUE OF SHIPMENTS (MILLIONS)
Cereal preparations	88	97	$ 793
Chewing gum	86	96	304
Cigarettes	81	100	3,045
Synthetic rubber	61	82	927
Soap and detergents	70	78	2,593
Tires and inner tubes	70	88	3,734
Flat glass	94	98	611
Primary aluminum	°	100	1,609
Metal cans	73	84	2,891
Steam engines and turbines	88	98	1,043
Typewriters	81	99	596
Transformers	65	78	1,188
Home laundry equipment	78	95	982
Electric lamps	91	95	782
Motor vehicles and parts	92	98	27,296
Locomotives and parts	97	99	690

° Withheld to avoid disclosure.
Source: U.S. Bureau of the Census, Census of Manufactures, 1967, *Special Report Series: Concentration Ratios in Manufacturing*, MC 67(S)-2.1, Part I, Table 1.

The production of ready-mixed concrete provides a good example of this disparity. In 1958, the 4-firm and 8-firm concentration figures were 4 percent and 7 percent respectively. There is, of course, no such thing as a national ready-mixed concrete market. Here, the SMSA is the most appropriate area, and a sample of 8-firm concentration ratios in 22 large selected SMSA's showed that, with the exception of one area, all were 50 percent or more.[25] In more than one-half of the areas, the 8-firm ratios were 75 percent or more.

A brief look at the identity of a few of the more highly concentrated industries in our economy suggests the substantial importance of these industries to the total manufacturing complex (see Table 2-7).

[24] Using an 8-firm concentration ratio of 50 percent or more as a definition of "monopoly" changes the picture considerably. These data show that in 1963, 199 of the 417 industries included (48 percent) had eight-firm concentration ratios of 50 percent or more.
[25] FTC, *Economic Report on Mergers and Vertical Integration in the Cement Industry*, 1966, p. 48.

Almost all of the industries in Table 2-7 have total shipments of one-half billion dollars or more. There are of course, many large industries in which the level of concentration is fairly low. The purpose of Table 2-7 is not to suggest that all large industries are highly concentrated, but that many of our highly concentrated industries are rather large in terms of total shipments. This is particularly true in our largest consumer goods industries, such as tires, soaps and detergents, cigarettes, and automobiles. Other data show, in addition, that between 1958 and 1967, the level of concentration increased in most of the industries which are included.[26]

Gross Changes in Concentration   Many concentration studies show in a simple manner the overall changes that have occurred between Census years. A recent study by the Federal Trade Commission depicted the changes which occurred in the level of concentration in a set of 215 comparable industries over the period 1947–1963. Comparable, in this sense, means that the industry definition has remained substantially the same over the period under examination. Thus, they involve the same coverage (see Table 2-8).

Table 2-8   Percentage Change in 4-Firm Concentration Ratios in 215 Comparable Industries: 1947–1954, 1954–1958, 1958–1963, and 1947–1963

AMOUNT OF CHANGE	1947–1954	1954–1958	1958–1963	1947–1963
Increase [a]	62	47	74	81
No change [b]	78	102	92	46
Decrease [c]	75	66	49	88
Total	215	215	215	215

[a] Increase of more than 3 percent.
[b] Plus or minus 3 percent.
[c] Decrease of more than 3 percent.
Source: W. F. Mueller, "Statement," *Hearings before the Senate Select Committee on Small Business*, March 15, 1967, p. 69.

Over the entire period, the industry changes in concentration just about offset one another: Concentration increased by three percent or more in 81, *or* 38 percent of the industries, but declined by the same amount in 88, *or* 41 percent of the industries. A closer look at the shorter periods suggests that the number of industries in which the level of concentration declined steadily from 35 percent in the 1947–1954 period to 23 percent in the 1958–1963 period. On the other hand, the number

[26] In 70 percent of the industries shown in Table 2-7 for which comparable data are available, the 4-firm concentration levels increased.

of industries which showed an increase between 1958 and 1963 is up over the earlier period.

Additional information useful to an analysis of concentration changes can be obtained from these same data if they are analyzed on the basis of the type of industry which is involved. For this purpose the industries have been divided into consumer goods and producer goods industries (see Table 2–9).

Table 2-9   Percentage Distribution of Changes in 4-Firm Concentration Ratios in 215 Comparable Industries, by Industry Type: 1947–1954, 1954–1958, 1958–1963, and 1947–1963

CONCENTRATION CHANGE	1947–1954	1954–1958	1958–1963	1947–1963
Consumer Goods[a]				
Increase	29	24	47	49
No change	36	46	41	17
Decrease	35	30	12	34
Producer Goods[b]				
Increase	28	20	24	28
No change	37	48	44	25
Decrease	35	32	32	47

[a] 95 consumer goods industries.
[b] 120 producer goods industries.
Source: W. F. Mueller, "Statement," *Hearings before the Senate Select Committee on Small Business,* March 15, 1967, p. 69.

This division of industries shows some changes not apparent from an examination of the gross changes alone. In particular, there is one shift that will be of considerable interest to us in discussing the effect of product differentiation in Chapter 3. Briefly stated, the data show that over the period 1947–1963, concentration in consumer goods industries increased in almost one-half of the industries, and declined in about one-third. In particular, they show that between 1958 and 1963 concentration increased in 47 percent of the industries, but declined in only 12 percent of the consumer goods industries. If these consumer goods industries constitute a representative sample, there has been a substantial increase in the level of concentration in these industries, particularly in the most recent period.

In producer goods industries, the situation is just the reverse. Between 1947 and 1963 concentration increased in 28 percent of the industries but decreased in 47 percent. Thus, concentration has increased in consumer goods industries but declined in producer goods industries during the postwar periods. Reference to even the limited number of industries included in Table 2–7 lends some weight to this point of view. In five of the seven producer goods industries for which data are available (synthetic rubber, primary aluminum, steam engines and turbines, metal cans, and transformers), concentration declined between 1958 and 1963. In the other two, locomotives and parts, and flat glass, concentration increased slightly, from 95 percent to 98 percent, and from 92 percent to 96 percent respectively.

Summary

Long as this examination of the measures and meaning of concentration may have been, it only scratches the surface of what can and has been undertaken by economists in their attempts to develop meaningful measures of the structure of American industry. Such measures should assist us in understanding and evaluating the results obtained in manufacturing industries.

What conclusions can be reached from this examination? In general, it is clear that overall manufacturing concentration has increased substantially since the end of World War II. Although the data for earlier periods are poor, it appears that we have reached an all time high in terms of the concentration of control of economic resources in the hands of the owners and managers of a relatively few large corporate concerns. The precise meaning of these changes is disputed, but these structural changes may be simply the forerunners of serious malfunctions in the operation of our competitive market economy: Non-competitive structure breeds non-competitive performance.

An examination of concentration at the industry level seems to suggest that this concern may be the figment of statistical manipulation. Data showing the trend of change over the postwar period show as many cases of decreasing concentration as of increasing concentration. If this is true, and if there are no important size differences in the increasing and decreasing areas, there may be no reason for concern. The limited analysis included here suggests that this may be a considerable oversimplification of the change.

The purpose of this examination has been two-fold: First, to acquaint the reader with the results of a limited number of studies of concentration, and to provide some feeling for the methods of analysis which may be employed and the manner in which the results may be shown. We have seen very general measures of concentration, as well as quite specific measures, (the level of concentration in the production of metal cans) and some which involve combination of the two (the trend of concentration in consumer goods industries versus producer goods industries). Second, an attempt has been made to suggest some interpretations which might be given to results from the study of concentration and some limitations which should be kept in mind in looking at gross measures of the change in industry structure. For example, not all industries are nation-wide in scope, thus particular care should be taken in the uncritical acceptance and use of nation-wide data in an analysis of essentially local or regional industries. No separate treatment of local market levels of concentration is included because of the extreme limitation of the available data in this area. Some data for smaller geographic markets are contained in *Concentration Ratios in Manufacturing Industry: 1963*, Part II. However, these data are presented on a state-wide basis, which is sometimes too small a market area, while in other cases (ready-mixed concrete, for example) it is much too large.

It is hoped that by this time the reader will have gained an appreciation of the extent of concentration which prevails in the manufacturing segment of our economy, as well as the trend of concentration over recent years. Since antitrust policy is a matter of national concern, an understanding of the ways in which structural changes affect the level of prices and profits, and consequently the number of alternatives available to buyers, is important.

CAUSES OF CONCENTRATION

Is the increase in concentration, which is apparent in many industries, a necessary consequence of technological change in the production and distribution of manufactured products, or are there better explanations of the changes noted in recent years? Many suggest that changing technology is the basic reason for such changes. Others suggest that the desire of large producers to enhance their economic power *vis à vis* their smaller competitors may be a better explanation of their growth. We will look at some of the evidence which has been developed to appraise the validity of these positions generally and in relation to specific industries. This analysis looks basically at changes in optimum scale of plant, rate of industry growth and the influence of merger activity on concentration. An understanding of the relative importance of these forces may provide some insights into what may be expected in the future.

Economies of Scale

One of the longest standing explanations of the increase in concentration has been the "economic of scale" argument. The arguments regarding the relative shape and position of long-run and short-run cost curve for the plant, suggest that as the scale of any plant is increased up to some point (output M for example), average costs of production tend to fall.

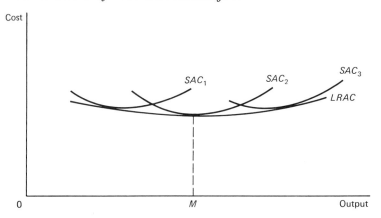

Figure 2-1   Short-Run and Long-Run Production Costs

Beyond output M, costs may rise (rapidly or slowly) or may remain the same, at least for an extended period. The same conclusions can be reached if distribution costs are added to production costs. Thus, it is obvious that costs tend to decline as the scale of output increases. Insofar as is known, this principle has general applicability.

One crucial question is ignored by this rather simple restatement of the influence of scale of output on costs. The important question, of course, concerns the level of industry output at which minimum average costs of production and distribution are reached. How large a share of total industry output must be accounted for by a plant or firm [27] before minimum costs are reached? In many industries, maximum scale economies are obtained with a very small share of industry output—perhaps as little as ½ of 1 percent. In other industries, a firm might have to account for as much as 25 to 30 percent of industry capacity before it achieves minimum costs of production.

> Ideally, empirical evidence on economies of scale should be obtained by observing the variations in costs associated with different scales of plant or firm *with all other cost influences constant.*[28]

It is obvious that it is not possible in the real world to find any such ideal situation. One cannot vary the scale of an operating plant in a time vacuum to determine the precise operating costs associated with different levels of output. There are many other problems which make this approach an unrealistic one. As a consequence, two alternative

[27] Technically speaking, economies of the firm differ slightly from economies of scale, which refer only to lower costs associated with the expansion of a given plant. For our purposes, the two will be used more or less interchangeably.

[28] Caleb A. Smith, "Survey of the Empirical Evidence on Economies of Scale," *Business Concentration and Price Policy*, National Bureau of Economic Research, New York, 1955, p. 200. Emphasis added.

methods have been developed to appraise the relationship between scale of plant and average costs of production.[29] These are referred to as the statistical and engineering approaches. In recent years, a third method has been added. This is the "survivor" method.

Statistical cost studies attempt to relate costs and scale for the different types of production processes employed in the production of some goods. If the only reason for choosing different production processes were the scale of plant then this kind of study would be sufficient. Unfortunately, there are other reasons. Moreover, statistical cost studies assume that the observed cost data available were obtained while the firm was operating at its most efficient (optimal) rate of output with any given scale of plant. Only if costs vary by a small amount at such observed outputs are the data obtained useful.

The engineering approach, on the other hand, examines each part of the production process to evaluate the technical relationship between inputs and outputs. The results of this analysis are then modified to take into account factor and product prices in arriving at an estimate of the most efficient scale of plant. As in all cases, efficiency must be discussed relative to the actual market conditions which face the firm.

The "survivor" approach alternative has been developed within the past ten years, principally by George Stigler.[30] In his criticism of the usefulness of the scale economies concept, Stigler suggests that we have been obsessed by a desire to develop a precise, objective measure of optimum size. Moreover, he claims that the necessary information has been available but we have failed to see it. In other words, the optimum scale of plant might be likened to the optimum length of one's legs. According to Stigler:

> The survivor technique proceeds to solve the problem of determining the optimum firm size as follows: Classify the firms in an industry by size, and calculate the share of industry output coming from each size class over time. If the share of a given class falls, it is relatively inefficient, and in general is more inefficient the more rapidly the share falls.[31]

As Stigler points out, this does not deal with the question of socially optimum size of plant or firm, since "the most efficient size of firm may arise from the possession of monopoly power, undesirable labor practices, discriminatory legislation, etc." [32] In other words, the most efficient size of firm or plant is that which evolves 'naturally' in an industry.

---

[29] The use of rate of return and cost level studies are both subject to the problem of asset evaluation. Rate of return studies are further suspect because they include not only profits related to efficiency, but those related to market power.

[30] George J. Stigler, "The Economies of Scale," *The Journal of Law and Economics*, October 1958, pp. 54–71.

[31] *Ibid.*, p. 55.

[32] *Ibid.*, p. 56.

Our primary interest is not in the development of measures of optimal firm size but in looking at the degree to which changing concentration in American industry can be explained by systematic changes in the scale economies. Irrespective of the method of measurement employed, the number of usable cost studies is small (although growing) given the fact that they constitute the results of two decades of research.

One of the better early studies of the relationship between cost and scale appeared in 1948.[33] In this study, Blair culled data from a number of sources—TNEC studies, OPA cost data, special studies by the FTC, and miscellaneous other studies. Many of the early studies obtained mixed results. For example, in his study of profitability prior to and following consolidation, Dewing concluded that the earnings of the separate plants before consolidation were greater than the earnings of the same plants following consolidation.[34] TNEC Monograph No. 27, using a method which constitutes a crude form of the survivor technique, presented a number of case studies showing industries in which the total share of output produced in large plants was increasing and others where it was declining. A 1945 study of large bakeries showed that the four largest firms had lower materials costs, but did not have the lowest unit costs of production. A similar study of tire manufacturers showed that the costs of the four largest tire producers exceeded those of ten other producers by between 6 percent and 21 percent, depending upon the tire size in question. Studies of mixed fertilizer and bulk phosphate production failed to show that lowest production costs were achieved by firms in the largest size classes. It should be pointed out that, in all of the studies where considerable detail is available, the very smallest producers always had the highest unit costs. In summary, Blair concluded that: "The long-term, general, and pervasive increase in plant size throughout most industries has come to an end." [35]

A later study of the application of the survivor technique to 89 industries by Saving [36] reaches these conclusions, among others: (1) The mean and minimum optimum size of plant is usually small when compared to the size of the industry; and (2) "Optimum size is *rarely* so large as to necessitate noncompetitive industry behavior." [37] These conclusions are reached despite the fact that optimum size is measured only in terms of private social cost. A partial list of the industries and their mean optimum size is shown in Table 2–10.

[33] John Blair, "Does Large-Scale Enterprise Result in Lower Costs: Technology and Size," *American Economic Review*, May 1948, pp. 121–152.
[34] A. W. Dewing, "A Statistical Test of the Success of Consolidations," *Quarterly Journal of Economics*, November 1921, pp. 90–94 *passim*.
[35] Blair, *op. cit.*, p. 151.
[36] T. J. Saving, "Estimation of Optimum Size of Plant by the Survivor Technique," *The Quarterly Journal of Economics*, November 1963, pp. 569–603.
[37] *Ibid.*, p. 597.

Table 2-10   Distribution of 89 American Manufacturing
Industries by Mean Optimum Size of Plant

SHARE OF INDUSTRY VALUE ADDED PRODUCED BY MEAN SIZE PLANT	NUMBER
0 to 0.9 percent	50
1.0 percent to 1.9 percent	20
2.0 percent to 2.9 percent	8
3.0 percent to 3.9 percent	5
4.0 percent to 4.9 percent	2
5.0 percent to 7.4 percent	3
7.5 percent to 9.9 percent	1
10.0 percent to 14.9 percent	1
15.0 percent and over	1

Source: T. R. Saving, "Estimation of Optimum Size of Plant by the Survivor Technique," *Quarterly Journal of Economics,* November 1963, pp. 598–602.

The data presented in Table 2–10 support Saving's contention with respect to the relatively small size of plant necessary to achieve substantial plant economies. In almost 60 percent of the industries examined, the optimum size was a plant with less than one percent of the industry's output. In one case, the mean optimum size in the industry accounted for less than .05 of 1 percent of the industry. The results obtained by Saving using the survivor technique are similar to those obtained by Bain through the use of a questionnaire sent to *the leading firms in twenty major industries.*[38] In some cases the Bain figures appear to be slightly higher. The Bain data clearly show that the actual level of concentration is considerably in excess of the size that would be dictated by scale requirements.

In a recent study, Blair looks at the changes which occurred between plant concentration and company concentration in 125 industries between 1947 and 1958.[39] The results of this study are interesting in light of apparent recent increases in company concentration. Plant concentration decreased in 67 industries, increased in 48 and remained the same in 10 others. On the other hand, company concentration increased in 57 industries, decreased in 56 and remained the same in 12. Thus, while

[38] Joe S. Bain, *Barriers to New Competition,* Harvard University Press, Cambridge, Mass., 1956, pp. 53–114.
[39] John Blair, "Statement," *Economic Concentration, Part 4—Concentration and Efficiency,* Hearings before the Senate Subcommittee on Antitrust and Monopoly, August 24, 1965, pp. 1536–1556.

company concentration appeared to remain unchanged in gross terms, plant concentration decreased substantially.

Many other studies of competitive conditions in a number of industries come to essentially the same results. Walter Mead [40] and a recent study by the Federal Trade Commission [41] came to much the same conclusions. Thus, all of these studies are unanimous: There is simply no evidence that the present level of concentration has been induced by scale considerations. Moreover, the evidence available suggests that the divergence between plant and company concentration has been increasing in recent years. Finally, there is no substantial amount of evidence that increases in concentration in the near future are likely to be induced by technological changes which require larger scale of plant.

The Effects of Merger on Concentration   Information which relates changes in concentration to merger activity is much more difficult to obtain. Studies of this type can only be obtained through careful and painstaking searching and analysis. Even then the results are not always unambiguous. Two recent studies by the Federal Trade Commission attempt to relate these two variables.[42] The marked reduction in the number and size of horizontal mergers in recent years suggests that studies such as these which measure the direct impact of merger will not be repeated in many other industries.

In general, these studies agree that merger activity in the past has added to *industry* concentration. The *Food Manufacturing* study, for example, shows not only the contribution of mergers to the increased market shares of the leading food manufacturers, but their dependence upon mergers for entry into new markets. Between 1950 and 1965, the share of the 50 largest [43] food manufacturers increased from 39.7 percent to 50.2 percent of total food industry assets.[44] A careful examination of the data show that merger activity accounted for 37 percent of the asset growth of the 50 largest firms. How important is that figure? The answer is simple: Had those firms not engaged in any merger activity, their share of total industry assets would have declined.

This study also looked at the number of new 4-digit industries which 25 of the largest food manufacturers entered over the same period. This examination showed that these 25 firms entered a total of 108 new indus-

[40] Walter J. Mead, "Statement," *Economic Concentration, Part 4—Concentration and Efficiency, op. cit.*, pp. 1630–1644.

[41] Federal Trade Commission, *Staff Report on the Structure of Food Manufacturing*, Technical Study No. 8, National Commission on Food Marketing, June 1966, pp. 83–99.

[42] FTC, *Staff Report on the Structure of Food Manufacturing, op. cit.*, and *Economic Report on Corporate Mergers, op. cit.*

[43] Largest in 1965.

[44] *Staff Report on the Structure of Food Manufacturing, op. cit.* p. 118.

tries over the 15 year period. Was this internal development or the result of an active merger policy? In this industry, merger proved to be by far the most significant source of entry. Almost 90 percent of the entry into new industries resulted from merger activity; only 13 of the 108 new industries were entered as a result of internal growth and development.

It is clear that active merger activity can change the contours of industry structure. In some industries, merger activity has been of little importance in recent years. In others, particularly those where relatively low levels of concentration have prevailed in the past, recent changes have occurred.

The recent *Report on Corporate Mergers* shows the impact of mergers during the past two merger movements. It shows, for example, that between 1925 and 1931 the share of total manufacturing assets held by the 100 largest corporations rose from 35.6 percent to 43.4 percent or 7.8 percent. The assets acquired by these companies accounted for 5.3 percent (or 68 percent of the increase).[45] Between 1948 and 1968, the assets of the 200 largest manufacturing firms increased by $242.4 billion. Approximately 20.6 percent of this total (or about $50 billion) was attributable to merger activity.[46] Between 1947 and 1968, the share of corporate manufacturing assets held by the 200 largest firms increased by 16.2 percent from 42.4 percent to 60.9 percent.[47] The *Report* estimates that 15.5 percentage points of this increase came from merger alone. Therefore, in the absence of their merger activity, they would have shown an increase in their share of only .7 of 1 percent over the 22 year period.

Concentration and Mobility   A number of studies have emphasized another aspect of structure which is intimately related to concentration—firm mobility. Kaplan, for example, pointed out that despite the fact that the level of concentration may remain the same, the adverse competitive impact associated with a particular level may be offset if the identity of the leading firms changes.[48] In other words, the lack of mobility may lead to adverse competitive effects.

Some recent studies suggest that while this may be true, most mobility which has existed in recent years has come about as a result of merger activity.[49] Also, the mobility which exists occurs among the smaller firms, not among the larger firms where gains in competition might be

---

[45] *Economic Report on Corporate Mergers, op. cit.*, p. 182.
[46] *Ibid.*, p. 186.
[47] *Ibid.*, p. 192.
[48] A. D. H. Kaplan, *op. cit.*, pp. 123–53.
[49] Stanley E. Boyle and Robert L. Sorensen, "Concentration and Mobility: An Alternative Measure of Industry Structure," *Journal of Industrial Economics*, April 1971.

obtained.[50] Other studies show that changes in concentration are inversely related to changes in mobility.[51]

As a consequence, these studies suggest that studies of mobility will not substitute for other examinations of industry structure.

SUMMARY

Does there appear to be any consistent pattern of change from the studies which have been referred to in this Chapter? For the most part, the answer is yes!

The data show that the level of general concentration (the share held by the 200 largest manufacturing firms) has increased by about one-third since 1940. The bulk of that increase occurred prior to 1958 with the exception of a recent spurt since 1966. The net result is that the level of concentration in manufacturing industries is at an all time high.

Using *Census of Manufactures* data for 215 comparable industries over the 1947–1963 period, Mueller showed that, in general, increases and decreases in concentration more or less offset one another. Concentration increased in industries and decreased in others. However, if the concentration changes are analyzed in terms of consumer goods and producer goods industries, definite patterns exist. Concentration has tended to increase in consumer goods industries and to decrease in producer goods industries. Other data show that industries which have relatively high levels of concentration appear to be rather large. That is not to say, however, that all large industries have high concentration.

The data presented raise certain questions regarding the relationship between the level and changes in concentration and the state of technology. A number of different measures have been used to measure the optimum size plant. Irrespective of the method employed, there is no evidence that present levels of concentration are required by present levels of scale economies. By any measure, concentration levels far exceed actual production scale requirements. What is responsible for the concentration changes noted? Clearly, a factor responsible for a portion of the increases in general concentration has been the substantial step-up in merger activity. At the individual industry level, increases in concentration seem to have occurred primarily in consumer goods industries.

[50] Stanley E. Boyle, "Large Industrial Corporations and Asset Shares: A Comment," *American Economic Review*, March 1971, pp. 163–167.

[51] Stanley E. Boyle and Joseph P. McKenna, "Size Mobility of 100 and 200 Largest American Manufacturing Corporations: 1919–64," *The Antitrust Bulletin*, Fall 1970, pp. 505–519.

The virtual disappearance of large horizontal mergers in the postwar period, particularly since 1955, suggests that we must seek another answer.

A part of that answer may be the increased importance of product differentiation activities (primarily advertising) by large consumer goods producers. The significance of this activity is looked at in some detail in Chapters 3 and 5.

3

THE STRUCTURE OF AMERICAN INDUSTRY: II

Until recently almost all studies of industry structure have been limited largely to the significance of the level, and changes in the level, of concentration. As a by-product, some of these studies have examined the causes of concentration within a rather narrow set of limits—most of them associated with technological changes in either production or distribution methods. Consequently, most of these early studies of the structure of industry have a decidedly one-dimensional nature. Moreover, the results obtained (in terms of whether or not the level of concentration in an industry is high, low or in the middle range) were affected by the point of measurement selected, a 4-, 8-, 20-, or 50-firm level. In 1967, for example, 102 industries had four-firm concentration ratios of 50 percent or more. On the other hand, 199 had an 8-firm concentration ratio of 50 percent or more.

The meaning to be attached to any given concentration level is, as has been pointed out, dependent upon the size distribution of firms within the industry.[1] The greater the degree of disparity in firm size, whatever the level of concentration, the greater will be the economic

---

[1] An interesting study of the relationship between the level of concentration of firms ranked 1 through 4, the marginal concentration of firms ranked 5 through 8, and industry performance is examined in Richard A. Miller, "Marginal Concentration Ratios and Industrial Profit Rates: Some Empirical Results of Oligopoly Behavior," *The Southern Economic Journal*, October 1967, pp. 259–267. As would be expected, the correlation between profits and the marginal concentration ratio of this group of firms is negative and significant.

power of the largest firms.[2] The rate and direction of growth may have
an effect on the long-run significance of any given level of concentration. This is particularly true if changes in industry growth are associated with changes in the number of firms in the industry.

Complex as the measurement problems may be, guidelines exist and
research has been undertaken which suggests the general types of relationships which can be expected as changes occur in these variables.[3] A
new dimension was added to the study of industrial organization in the
middle-1950s as a result of the publication of an epic work by Bain. This
book, *Barriers to New Competition*, and the articles which preceded it
demonstrated the necessity to include an analysis of product differentiation as a distinct structural characteristic of product markets. Others
had recognized that promotional activities are engaged in by firms in
the hope of altering buyer preferences toward their product and away
from those of their rivals. These may occur irrespective of the actual differences (and they may be substantial) between their outputs.

> The great increase in the amount of advertising in the past century and
> the apparent prosperity of most companies that have advertised persis-
> tently may be accepted as evidence that advertising benefits those who
> use it.[4]

Although this statement was made 45 years ago, it represents much
current thinking on the subject. We assume that effective promotional
activities affect both the slope and the position of the demand curve facing the firm in an imperfectly competitive industry. We assume, also
that it may affect the industry demand curve by shifting it to the right.

Prior to the appearance of *Barriers to New Competition*, discussions of
the economic significance of advertising were limited to such general
considerations. The knowledge that product differentiation, by itself, affects the demand for some products provides less than a complete picture. Bain's analysis provides that necessary additional ingredient. It
suggests the ways in which it is possible to measure the economic significance of such activities and to appraise their competitive impact. It
suggests the impact of such activities upon industry structure, and allows for the systematic examination of such activities as an important
aspect of firm conduct.

For the most part, the remainder of this chapter is devoted to the

[2] William Fellner, "Comment," *Business Concentration and Price Policy*, National
Bureau of Economic Research, New York, 1954, pp. 113–116.
[3] General studies are somewhat limited in number, but the reader may be interested in William G. Sheppard, "Trends of Concentration in American Manufacturing
Industries," *The Review of Economics and Statistics*, May 1964, pp. 200–212.
[4] G. B. Hotchkiss, "An Economic Defense of Advertising," *The American Economic Review*, March 1925, p. 14.

competitive significance of product differentiation.[5] A brief recital of the sources of product differentiation and the theoretical consequences of its existence is followed by an examination of the results of a limited number of empirical studies of the incidence and significance of product differentiation as a structural variable. These areas involve an analysis of the relationship between concentration and product differentiation.

SOURCES OF PRODUCT DIFFERENTIATION

By degree of product differentiation, we refer to "the extent to which buyers differentiate, distinguish, or have specific preferences among the competing outputs of various sellers established in an industry." [6] These are activities which are undertaken by the manufacturer or seller in the hope of convincing the consumer that the outputs of all other producers are poor substitutes for his. Some of the differences may be real. One producer develops a new product, or an interesting and significant variation of an existing class of products. Thus, he establishes, at least for a short period of time, a market which is his own. As others adjust their products, sales methods and/or prices to meet the product characteristics of that of the innovator, the differences become less real and more imagined.

Other promotional activity is based on the premise that the consumer can be persuaded to buy almost anything. There seems to be an endless variety of forms that this persuasion may take, and it may have a number of different but related goals. For example, it may be directed to create a desire on the part of the buyer for a particular product (product promotion). It may attempt to associate a given brand name, trademark, or producer's name with an assumed level of quality for all products which carry this identification (image promotion). Or it may be designed simply to confuse the consumer regarding the accuracy of relative merits and characteristics of the product of competing manufacturers. Whatever the ostensive goal or the form of the appeal, one is tempted to agree with the observation made almost 40 years ago that "the primary economic function of advertising is to stimulate or control

[5] In addition to the physical differences and promotional claims regarding the distinction between products, other product differentiation aspects significantly affect competition between firms. Two classes of these cover differences between sales methods employed by different firms, as well as the location and identity of the dealer handling the product. The inability of sellers to establish a viable independent retail distribution network has resulted directly in the failure of new entrants. This is a particularly important factor in the sale of automobiles.

[6] Joe S. Bain, *Industrial Organization*, 2nd ed., New York, John Wiley & Sons, Inc., 1968, p. 223.

consumption." [7] Some product differentiation activities, notably advertising, make buyers aware of the availability of products or particular characteristics of products which they might otherwise ignore. Such activities result in both private and social gains. In discussions of the benefits which come to consumers, one question is often asked: What share of total promotional activities are actually devoted to such informational programs? A suspicion exists in minds of many that the share is not great. Unfortunately, data are not available which can yield precise answers on either side of this issue.

Brand name advertising is a particularly interesting phenomenon. It has been used in a variety of ways and for a number of purposes. Such promotion is aimed at convincing the buyer that the products of a given seller are basically of a uniform and usually superior quality (or relatively superior at some price) than those of other competing sellers, irrespective of the particular merits of the product in question. In other words, it is an appeal not to reason but to emotion. It is certainly not new. For years, DuPont put out its relentless message "Better Things for Better Living Through Chemistry." It was not an invitation to compare the merits of its products on an individual basis; rather, it was a repeated statement in the praise of all products produced by that firm. Our laws are quite explicit in their protection of trademarks and trade names. Given the fact that producers spend billions of dollars promoting them each year, there is little doubt that they are valuable property.

Many if not most brand name promotional activities tend to associate the name with quality, and the quality with a higher price. This relationship is sometimes explicitly stated, sometimes merely implied. It is a relationship, moreover, which the small buyer has little hope of actually confirming. He is in no position to test the truth or falsity of such claims. In many instances they are true, but a number of studies have demonstrated that there is not necessarily a high and positive correlation between price and product quality. A careful examination of any issue of *Consumer Reports* confirms this observation.

In the final instance, brand name advertising is like religion—you either have the faith or not and no amount of explanation or testing will substitute for it.

An additional source of product differentiation is ignorance on the part of consumers as to the quality and performance characteristics of the products they buy. This is true for almost all buyers and for almost all products purchased. It is commonly assumed that consumers are less ignorant regarding smaller products they purchase daily than they are

---

[7] Collis A. Stocking, "Modern Advertising and Economic Theory," *The American Economic Review*, March 1931, p. 50.

regarding products like large appliances, furniture and automobiles which they purchase infrequently. There is no evidence that this is necessarily true. In fact, what evidence there is suggests that consumer ignorance with respect to items purchased daily is quite high.[8] The basic difference, if one exists, is with regard to how ignorant we are about different products.

The average consumer, compared with the average industrial buyer, has little useful technical knowledge regarding the physical or other properties of the products he purchases.[9] For example, what percent of ordinary consumers understands clearly the relative merits of "hand wired" versus "printed" circuits in electronic appliances compared with their respective costs? Claims are made on both sides of the argument. Such supposed technical material is even included in advertising material, but to what purpose? To clarify or to confuse? Since the average consumer is not equipped to sort out the relative advantages and disadvantages of each production technique, such technical explanations tend to obscure the issue and confuse him. Industrial purchasers are able to assess the merits (technical and qualitative) of products they purchase. As a consequence, promotional expenditures in trade papers and magazines are quite small. If the differences between products were real, and the supposed advantages really existed, what better place (in sales to large volume purchasers) to point them out?

In recent years, a number of naive suggestions have been made that an organization be established which would be composed of interested businessmen and representatives of the consuming public. This organization would take the lead in the establishment of voluntary quality and performance standards for consumer products. Needless to say, such an organization has never come to pass and it never will. The reasons are simple. American companies and trade associations spend somewhere in the vicinity of $18 billion a year (1968) to convince the consuming public that the firm or group of firms is producing a product or products with unique characteristics. These efforts have met with considerable success. In effect, therefore, this proposal suggests that those who have engaged in successful product differentation give up the bulk of this type of activity, as well as the gains they have achieved, all in the name of greater consumer welfare.

---

[8] In recent years, the Federal government has taken increased notice of attempts to deceive consumers. Since 1966, The Federal Commission has published a number of reports which deal with various aspects of this problem. These include *Staff Report to the FTC on Cents-Off Promotions in the Coffee Industry*, 1966; *Staff Report on Automobile Warranties*, 1968; *Economic Report on Installment Credit and Retail Sales Practices of District of Columbia Retailers*, 1968; and *Economic Report on the Use of Games of Chance in Food and Gasoline Retailing*, 1968.

[9] Tibor Scitovsky, *Welfare and Competition*, Homewood, Ill., Richard D. Irwin, Inc., 1951, pp. 423–425.

Whatever the sources of product differentation and reasons advanced by sellers, the fact remains that buyers believe that a considerable range of differences exists between the individual products in a given product class. Moreover, they are willing to pay price differentials for products which reflect such differentials. Thus, the economist is faced with the fact these promotional activities have, in fact, altered the demand for the product. Consumers pay 5 cents a half gallon more for Clorox than they will for almost all other $5\frac{1}{4}$ percent hyperchlorite solution liquid bleaches. The fact that they are all chemically identical is irrelevant. From an analytical standpoint they are a somewhat different product.

THE CONSEQUENCES OF PRODUCT DIFFERENTIATION

As we have seen, the term product differentiation is used basically as a shorthand way of describing a product market situation in which imperfections exist.[10] In markets, competitive or otherwise, where the outputs of all producers are viewed as perfect substitutes, price differentials do not exist. Thus, price uniformity, a necessary but not sufficient condition of a competitive market, exists in all markets characterized by homogeneity of product. As long as there are no appreciable gaps in product substitutability, price uniformity exists. Once product preferences develop, price differentials come as a natural consequence. An interesting consequence of this phenomenon is an explanation of the ways in which firm sizes are determined in homogeneous and nonhomogeneous product markets. In the first case, firm size becomes a combination of the presence of scale economies, if any, and historical accident —the selection of a certain plant location, the time of entry into the market or any of a dozen or more motives.[11] Where product differentials exist, on the other hand, differing firms sizes are also the result of the relative success of the firm in developing substitution gaps between its product and those of its major competitors. Many of the methods employed were discussed in the preceding section.

Given the presence of substitution gaps in a product market, let us look briefly at the theoretical impact of product differentiation upon market conduct and performance. The obvious impact of the structure of

[10] It might just as well be used to describe a discontinuous geographic market with sellers placed at uneven intervals from buyers. In such a situation, nearer sellers are always at an advantage in dealing with buyers in their own market areas. Distance (even in the case of homogeneous products) is translated into cost differentials, that is, production cost plus transportation. The nearer seller can, at least in theory, charge any price short of that of his nearest rival and retain his hold on his own market.

[11] If scale economies are unimportant, the market structure is effectively competitive. If scale or one of the other reasons is quite important, the resulting market structure is essentially that of a homogeneous oligopoly, for example, steel, copper, aluminum, synthetic rubber, and the like.

such an industry is to impede entry as a result of the fact that the outputs of all sellers are no longer perfect substitutes for each other. If preferences develop, the apparent effect is to reduce the effective size of the market available to other existing firms and to those contemplating entry into the industry. In the short run, a part of the market is foreclosed. If the market is large and the number of such firms is relatively small and/or the relative size of the market subject to such preferences is not large, the economic impact of strong product differentiation as a restriction on entry is small. However, if the reverse is true, it may result in a substantial impairment of entry conditions.

Product Differentiation and Conduct

Economic theory suggests that the effective segmentation of the market may result in predictable changes in the conduct of firms. These effects can be detected in such apparently unrelated areas as pricing behavior and patterns (including the persistence of price differentials), product performance (changes in the apparent form and design of the product), and the magnitude and intensity of promotional activities. In each area, certain *a priori* expectations may be anticipated as the extent of product differentiation increases.

Pricing Behavior   It is often said that firms in competitive markets have no price policy. The absence of product differentials results in overall market prices being established by the forces of supply and demand. Each firm in such a market attempts to maximize its profits at any short-run price level. In doing this the firm is left with one basic decision—how much of the product it will produce. As a practical matter, however, this process does not provide an acceptable explanation of the pricing problems which beset the firm in actual markets. With the presence of substitution gaps different prices prevail within any given product market. This fact raises a number of interesting questions. How, for example, do firms, particularly leading firms, decide upon the level of their prices? What determines the extent of the price differentials between firms producing in the same product market? Under what conditions will firms engage in systematic or sporadic price discrimination?

We will ignore the question of whether or not firms, in fact, do attempt to maximize their profits as the traditional marginal pricing model contends. Let us assume, for the sake of argument, that the leading firms do hold to such a goal,[12] and that they behave in a manner which will result in achieving this goal.[13]

---

[12] In their *Pricing in Big Business*, Washington, D.C., The Brookings Institution, 1958, Kaplan, Dirlam and Lanzilloti contend that large firms are motivated by many other goals, some economic, some psychological. According to them, some firms set prices in accordance with some overall "target rate of return" while others follow a variety

Most discussions of pricing practices and behavior in oligopolistic markets assume, at least implicitly, the presence of some form of tacit understanding between the dominant firms in the industry. It is argued that as a result of these understandings, leading firms in an industry tend to move quite cautiously when making price changes, particularly price reductions, for fear their rivals will interpret their price changes as a prelude to an overt attempt to increase market share through direct price competition. Although product differentiation is generally referred to as a form of nonprice competition, one effect of *successful* product differentiation may be to increase the permissible range of independent pricing policy on the part of the firm. As the gaps between products of industrial firms increase, so may the extent of independent price policy. In theory, at least, the opportunity exists for greater price variation without retaliation than is the case where a high degree of homogeneity exists among the outputs of different sellers.[14]

In a situation where considerable product differentiation exists it is reasonable to assume that the leading firm, for example, will correctly conclude that the demand for its product is somewhat more inelastic than that facing its rivals. Stated more simply, this means that it can raise the price of its product above the level which prevails for other sellers and retain its market, or alternatively that it can make substantial inroads on the markets of its rivals by reducing its price.

One result of the discontinuity in product characteristics, is that each firm which succeeds in achieving substantial product differentiation is faced by its own individual demand curve. The curves of industry members may coincide, they may intersect or they may exist separately and distinctly from each other, D_1 and D_2 for example. (Figure 3-1) Those firms which have not been successful in differentiating their products are faced with somewhat more elastic (D_3) demand curves similar to those facing the firm in a competitive market. Again their primary decision is the quantity of the good they will produce given the size of the

---

of motivations. Others suggest that firms use some form of "average cost" or "full cost" pricing, a kind of cost plus arrangement. Recently, Baumol has even suggested that firms behave as if to maximize their sales. While some of these arguments have merit, they are left for discussion at a more appropriate occasion. His and a number of alternative approaches are discussed in: Duncan Bailey and Stanley E. Boyle, "Sales Revenue Maximization: An Empirical Vindication," paper presented at the meetings of the Southern Economic Association, November 1970, pp. 1–18.

[13] See for example, James S. Earley, "Marginal Policies of 'Excellently Managed' Companies," *American Economic Review*, March 1956, pp. 44–70. On the basis of the returns from a lengthy questionnaire sent to a large group of large corporations, Earley contended that firms do, in fact, make pricing, investment, product innovations, and other decisions in a manner consistent with the marginal model.

[14] The first test of this hypothesis is contained in Stanley E. Boyle and Charles R. McKnew, "The Impact of Product Differentiation Upon Price Flexibility in 63 Highly-Concentrated Consumer Product Classes: 1947–1969," *Proceedings of the Business and Economic Statistics Section of the American Statistical Association*, New York, December 1969.

unrestricted market (that part not held by firms with highly differentiated products). Given the differing demand curves facing individual firms (D_1, D_2, and D_3), each of which is attempting to maximize its profits, the most reasonable result to expect is a product market with persistent price differentials.

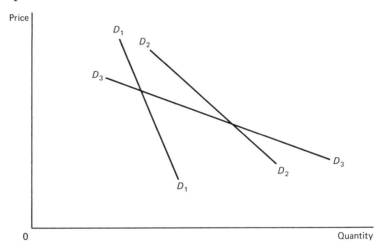

Figure 3-1   Individual Firm Demand with Product Differentiation

What will happen if some firm (with demand D_3) attempts either to raise or lower its prices unilaterally? The answer is not clear. Depending upon the relative size of the market held by the leading firms in the industry, different reactions may occur. If the price cutter is a relatively small national or regional firm it is unlikely that its action will have any substantial effect upon *either* the prices charged *or* the output of the leaders.[15] If, on the other hand, it is large enough to represent a serious threat to the existing leaders, its price reductions, even with a high degree of product differentiation, may evoke retaliatory price reductions by the industry leaders. One of the problems of the small firm in such an industry is to determine the range of price changes they may undertake without inviting retaliation. If the leading firms lower their prices in response to the initial price cut, the net effect is then a shifting downward of the entire pattern of prices.

[15] Since the demand facing producers with undifferentiated products tends to be more elastic than those who have been more successful, a portion of the increased sales going to the low price firm will come from buyers who have not been in the market for the product in question. Most discussions of this point implicitly assume that the increased sales going to the undifferentiated firms will be at the expense of other existing firms. The more successful they have been in differentiating their product, the more unlikely will be this result. It is illogical to assume that there is a given "fund" which is available for purchase of any product. The relative impact, of course, would depend upon the actual cross-elasticities of demand.

Many examples exist where persistent price differentials between products are the rule. Many of these fall in areas which we deal with every day. These include automobiles, small household appliances, laundry equipment, television sets, processed foods, some types of cleaning supplies, clothing and a variety of other products. The range of prices tends to be quite small in low price items, but to expand as the unit price of the product goes up.

	PRODUCT *A*	PRODUCT *B*
Firm A	$.37	$232
Firm B	.35	219
Firm C	.32	200

On the other hand, the relative range of prices is the same in the two examples. The difference between 32 cents and 37 cents is approximately 16 percent; the same difference between $200 and $232. It is interesting to note that many of the products listed are those for which consumers have difficulty in establishing and measuring quality differentials.

Thus, the presence of product differentiation substantially affects the pricing behavior of at least the more successful firms in the industry. It certainly allows for greater price flexibility than is true in homogeneous oligopoly. These are not the only aspects of interfirm price behavior which affect market competition; however, a more extended discussion of such practices as price discrimination, "administered prices" and the like is reserved for Chapter 4.

Product Competition   The presence of effective product differentiation may result in forms of competition other than direct price competition. A common form of nonprice competition is in the actual design and performance of the product. This competition may take a number of different forms. First, product competition may result in an increase in the rate of the introduction of new models. Second, competition in this area may take the form of a proliferation of models of a particular product. Third, sellers may place considerable emphasis on the development of extensive service facilities, thereby emphasizing their ability to provide superior and more comprehensive service.

How important is product competition? Here we are speaking for the most part of improvements in the quality, appearance or performance of existing products. A number of suggestions have been made in recent years that this form of competition has become increasingly important. Moreover, it is asserted that this type of product differentiation at the same time has increased the barriers to entry in industries where significant product differentiation exists *and* has increased the difficulties of survival facing smaller, less financially capable firms. In some circles this supposed drive to shorten the effective life of the product or product formulation has been referred to as planned obsolescence. In some industries, the annual introduction of new models of products or new forms of products has become an accepted method of competitive behavior. Here the desire is twofold. First, to convince the buyer that the product he is presently using is out of date, although it may have been the best made at the time he purchased it; second, to convince buyers that the seller's products have newer and better characteristics not contained in the products of his competitors.

In almost all cases, such activities are quite legitimate. Many buyers receive pleasure from the possession of the newest, most up-to-date model or form of the product; therefore, this type of competition enables him to fulfill his desire. Also, it is an extremely important form of competition for the newcomer into a market. One of the best forms of competitive pressure on firms in markets is the actual or potential threat that someone else will "build a better mousetrap."

On the other hand, some have found in this type of competition an insidious form of attack on small firms. Allegations have been made that leading companies in an industry, automobiles for example, have adopted rapid model introduction as a systematic and devious program to eliminate smaller and financially less viable competitors. In the production of durable goods, the producer must not only compete with the output of other firms but with a second-hand market which includes his own prior sales. This may well explain why planned obsolesence is more an accepted fact in durable goods production.

Rapid changes in product occur in other areas. In the drug industry, for example, many have suggested that the bulk of the changes which have been made in the composition of basic antibiotics by large "patent-holding" drug companies have been made with the idea in mind of eliminating smaller producers through the introduction of supposed newer and better drugs. At the same time it is suggested that medical practitioners are relatively insensitive to the differences, if any, which may exist between new and old formulations and will cheerfully prescribe whatever the drug salesmen recommend—brand name and all.

Some of these charges are obviously false. Economic theory and the simple psychology of business would indicate that if the introduction of a newer or better (they are not necessarily the same) product will improve a seller's position in the market, he will attempt to introduce such a product. In the automobile case particularly, there is much testimony which indicates that the cost of product design and innovation, while very important, was neither the sole nor the major determinant for the decline in the number of automobile manufacturers. Poor distribution organization, poor product design and other reasons were all responsible for their eventual demise. In the case of the drug industry, many of the allegations would appear to have substantial factual basis.

The cigarette industry offers another illustration of intensive activity in the introduction and promotion of new types and brands of cigarettes following the release of the first reports linking cigarette smoking to lung cancer and other diseases in the early 1950s. In 1952, for example, filter and menthol sales accounted for only 4.2 percent of all cigarette sales. Now they account for more than 60 percent of all sales, and with the switch from regular, unfiltered, unmentholated cigarettes has come a proliferation of new brands. These few examples suggest that in many highly concentrated markets where significant product differentiation exists, considerable attention will be devoted to the promotion and development of "new" brands and models.

Closely related to the practice of the introduction of new models of products at an increasing rate is that of introducing a whole series of highly related but supposedly distinct products. Automobiles again provide an interesting example of this practice. A few years ago, there were the Ford, Mercury, and Lincoln; the Chevrolet, Pontiac, Oldsmobile, Buick, and Cadillac; and the Plymouth, Dodge, DeSoto, Chrysler, and Imperial. Each represented a clear and distinct product line, at least to the automobile buyer, each with discernible price and product characteristics. Those days have disappeared forever. Some of the brand names have been discontinued. In other cases, a single brand name is used for a wide range of products. In earlier years, distinctions within each name were made on the basis of body style and the number of cylinders. Those easy days are gone forever.

Now the number of individually named models within each product line defies imagination. Each model represents a separate price line with considerable price and quality overlap between broad product lines, for example, between Chevrolets and Pontiacs. One might raise some interesting but not too significant questions about the sense of this whole process if the differences between the brands within the product line were real. If the differences are not real then one might raise some questions regarding the form of competition as being simply another method of attempting to confuse the already befuddled buyer. In either case, one would suspect that for the most part these efforts will continue and intensify wherever it is possible to exploit actual or imagined gradations in the performance characteristics of a product. Depending upon the success of the seller to quantify these differences, price differentials may develop.

A final form of product competition which will be discussed at this point is the emphasis upon the quality and general availability of service facilities as an aspect of product differentiation. The earliest form of these activities was the ability and integrity of the seller in being able to repair defects in the products sold. Associated with this was the performance guarantee attached to a product. Thus, if the product was sold as a unit (without parts) like a tire, or if it was so complex that it required specialized repair techniques known only to the producer or his agent, it could be returned for a new product or for qualified repair. It is obvious that a seller with a widely dispersed organization which handles such problems at points near to almost all consumers has a distinct advantage if he can convince the buyer that his specialized, rather than others' more generalized service is required in the event of malfunction. Obviously, the more expensive the product and the more expensive the cost of repair the more important and profitable this device becomes to the manufacturer and his designated dealers. As a consequence, this has become an important competitive device in the sale of automobiles, electrical appliances, tires and other products.

Small tire manufacturers have complained, for example, that they have been foreclosed from selling their tires in the original equipment market, in part because of the assertion of the major producers that they alone are able to provide rapid nation-wide service in the event that original equipment tires should prove defective in any manner. It is argued then that smaller or regional producers would be unable to carry out the necessary replacement function rapidly. If they were to succeed in breaking into the original equipment market on any large scale, this supposed shortcoming could presumably be overcome. In fact, it seems a trivial argument at best. It resembles the argument made by automobile manufacturers with respect to the necessity for highly controlled franchised dealers to handle the maintenance of their automobiles. At best, both arguments are irrelevant to the major purpose of such arrangements—the rigid control of all outlets. Automobile manufacturers show considerable ingenuity in this area. One of the most recent, the 50,000 mile guarantee providing all maintenance is in franchised or approved establishments, would tend to eliminate independent repair facilities if major automobile producers were to adopt and successfully enforce such provisions.

These devices as well as others have been employed by sellers in areas characterized by high product differentiation. These are the consequence of the nature of the structure of such markets. Some of these efforts may give desirable results; the gradations of demand between similar products are numerous and there is no basic reason why consumer desires in a free market economy should be pressed into a few undifferentiated and sometimes unappealing molds. Where firms have been successful in distinguishing their output from those of their competitors a necessary result is the proliferation of different but highly related products.

At the same time, this type of competition allows the unscrupulous seller the opportunity to take advantage of the usually uninformed buyer at his weakest point—the technical differences between any given product and its rivals. It is reasonable to expect, therefore, that many of the "new" products are not new, that many of the "different" products are not different, and that many of the "better" products are not better. In fact, some products may have none of these characteristics.

Product Promotion Activities   It is logical that efforts devoted to physical differentiation of products will be associated, in large measure, with efforts to promote the sales of the same product. Customers will not beat a path to your door simply because you build a better mousetrap. First, you have to convince the buyer that you have the superior mousetrap. Second, you must convince him that he needs not only a mousetrap but the best one available (at a price he is able to pay). Thus, with product differentiation an entire class of expenditures come into being —product promotion. It goes without saying, therefore, that *ceterus paribus* total costs also increase. Average total costs may, of course, decline if increased sales and any resulting economies of production offset the higher costs brought about by sales promotion.

Since product differentiation would appear to be a direct result of successful sales promotion activity, two rather obvious relationships might be expected between such expenditures and sales. First, it might be expected that products which had achieved, or whose producers were trying to achieve, considerable product differentiation would show a rather high promotion cost to sales ratio. In these areas some have suggested that there well may be a direct relationship between the success of such efforts (measured in terms of size and/or change in market share) and the relative magnitude of such expenditures. This is a matter of some dispute, but we will look at some of the evidence in Chapter 4. Thus, it might happen that larger firms in differentiated industries would have proportionately higher promotion expenditures than would smaller sellers.

The cynic might suggest that there is an inverse relationship between the actual difference in the product and the amount of money expended to sell it. This philosophy requires the presence of two rather unlikely conditions. First, it is necessary to suggest that all buyers are rather stupid and second that they will believe whatever they are told. It is true that buyers are not equipped to appraise the qualities of many products they purchase; it is doubtful, however, that advertising is that persuasive. If it were, sellers might be well advised to devote almost all of their activities to sales promotion and ignore product development.

We are left with two basic questions: How effective are advertising expenditures? To what extent do they enhance barriers to entry into markets? We will now turn our attention to these questions.

Product Differentiation and Performance

The assessment of industry performance in recent years has revolved largely about the question of the degree to which successful differentiation has resulted in higher profit levels. In other words, have firms, particularly the leading firms, producing differentiated products reaped the rewards of their efforts? Have they in fact achieved a partial monopoly position and the monopoly profits which economic theory suggests will be associated with this position? If these efforts have been successful, firms in such markets would have higher profits than elsewhere. Moreover, there might well be a predictable relationship between profitability and the degree of product differentiation within any given market. The more successful firm would then enjoy higher profits than others in the same industry. The literature in this area provides an interesting story by itself and will be examined in some detail in Chapter 5.

The Extent of Product Differentiation: Some Empirical Observations

How are product differentiation advantages measured? How important is product differentiation in different markets within the economy? These are extremely important questions. Unfortunately, the answers are not precise. There is no well-defined body of data which measures the substitution gaps between the outputs of different producers, theoretical discussions of the importance of cross-elasticity coefficients notwithstanding. No individual, group of individuals or agency of the Federal government has ever been in a position to amass such data. Thus, the answer to the first of the questions is, "not with much precision."

The absence of precise data does not mean that no way exists to measure the presence of product differentiation. As we have indicated already, many forms of product differentiation are dependent upon continued ignorance on the part of the buyer. Once buyers become accurately informed as to precise nature of differences between products, they cease to behave differently toward them in many instances. It goes without saying, therefore, that firms in almost all industries in which product differentiation is significant are engaged in the production of consumer goods, or in dealing with consumers. In this sense, manufacturing as well as most trade and service activities involves significant amounts of product differentiation. In these cases, sellers attempt to distinguish their outputs on the basis of quality, geographic location and the inclusiveness of their service. There are many advantages in being able to supply a full range of services or products to meet the diverse demands of buyers.

In almost all other areas, product differentiation is of relatively small importance. Agriculture, mining, nonresidential housing, communications, transportation, public utilities and most financial areas are, for the most part, without effective product differentiation. In almost all of these areas, the principal buyers of the product or service are well-informed. These buyers are interested in obtaining a product which meets certain specifications, and these standards can usually be met by a variety of sellers. The buyer is interested in achieving minimum costs.

A ton of copper ore, 100 bushels of No. 2 red wheat, or 1,000 feet of quarter inch copper wire with a covering of certain thickness, material and quality can all be produced or supplied by many sellers in the individual markets. This is also true of products which, when sold to noninstitutional buyers, lose their individual product differentiation characteristics. If a restaurant wishes to buy frozen peas of a certain size and quality, it doesn't really care who packs them. Its customers are not impressed by the identity of the packer; they care only whether the peas that accompanied their dinner were of an appropriate quality. The same is true for products like automobiles, tires, gasoline, detergents, drugs and medicines, and many others.

The best study of the importance of product differentiation is Bain's *Barriers to New Competition.* In this study of some 20 or more manufacturing industries, Bain categorized each according to the importance (great, moderate, and slight or negligible) of product differentiation and the specific sources of such advantages. A portion of Bain's results are compressed in Table 3-1.

Although this is far from a complete list of the major industries, it suggests the type of products which tend to have a high degree of product differentiation, as well as those in which it is considerably less important. A number of factors are mentioned by Bain and others which induce successful product differentiation. One fact is crystal clear, however: Almost all successful attempts to achieve a high degree of product differentiation are associated with extensive advertising activity. We might develop a rule that applies to all those hoping to achieve substantial differentiation. "Extensive advertising is necessary to achieve a high degree of product differentiation, *but* it will not assure it." It is, then, a necessary but not sufficient condition of success.

Real questions arise regarding the allegiance of buyers in such markets. How strong is their preference for a given product or set of products? Here there are no simple answers. For example, Table 3-1 shows the cigarette industry to be highly differentiated. It does not suggest the customer losses that the leading firm in the industry, R. J. Reynolds (Camels, Salem and Winston), would experience if its rivals were to drop their price by one, two, or five cents a package. They would probably lose a substantial quantity of sales. In most industries, in fact, the strength of the product differentiation is measured in terms of the price differential the leading firm can command without substantial losses in market share. This is true, for example, in canned fruits and vegetables, which Bain suggests show only a slight degree of product differentiation. Therefore, in some cases, product differentiation permits price differentials (canned fruits and vegetables). In others, price identity leads to product differentiation as the only way to allocate sales among different producers (cigarettes).

Table 3-1   The Significance and Source of Production Differentiation in Selected Industries

INDUSTRY	SOURCE OF PRODUCT DIFFERENTIATION
A. Great Product Differentiation	
Cigarettes	advertising
Fountain pens (quality)	advertising
Liquor	advertising
Typewriters	advertising, product design
Heavy Farm Machinery	product design, distribution system
Automobiles	advertising, product reputation, distribution system
B. Moderate Product Differentiation	
Soap	advertising
Rubber tires	advertising, distribution system
Specialty canned fruit and vegetable	advertising
Flour, consumer sales	advertising
Men's shoes, quality	advertising
Petroleum refining	advertising, distribution system
Metal containers	service, product control
C. Slight or Negligible Product Differentiation	
Shoes, lower price	advertising, distribution system
Canned fruits and vegetables	advertising
Gypsum products	established brand name
Meat products, processed	advertising
Light farm machinery	distribution system
Copper	customer inertia
Rayon	customer inertia
Steel	customer inertia, service
Cement	customer inertia
Fountain pens, low priced	customer inertia
Flour, industrial	customer inertia

Source: Compiled from Joe S. Bain, *Barriers to New Competition*, Cambridge, Mass., Harvard University Press, 1956, pp. 127–129.

Most empirical studies of product differentiation have shown a positive and significant relationship between the degree of product differentiation and the level of concentration. In most instances where the degree of product differentiation is high the level of concentration is high also. The reverse is not always true, since there are many reasons for the development of high levels of concentration other than product differentiation. These include scale economies, raw materials control, size of the market, outright collusion and patent restrictions.

The high level of concentration in the industries shown in Part A of Table 3-1 is substantial. The 4-firm concentration ratios for each of the industries included are in excess of 50 per cent and the average for the six industries is about 70 percent. As a group, therefore, they would have to be referred to as highly concentrated industries. Concentration levels are high also in the industries in Part B. However, they are slightly lower, on the average, than those in Part A. The industries contained in Part C show a substantial mixture of high and low levels of concentration; however, most of the instances where concentration levels are high are associated with raw materials control in basic industries. A number of studies which examine the association between product differentiation activities and concentration levels will be examined in the next chapter. Many of them are fragmentary but the results obtained in this area seem to be consistent.

Condition of Entry

In Chapters 2 and 3 considerable attention has been devoted to an examination of the structural factors most important in determining the conduct and performance of firms. In essence, however, all of the factors mentioned relate to the competitive relationships between firms already established in industries. These factors affect the nature of the competitive drives between existing industry members.

This ignores, however, the competitive importance of firms not in an industry at any given time. This is sometimes referred to as the strength of potential competition. How important a force is such "potential" competition insofar as it may effect the actual conduct and performance of sellers in a market area? The strength of potential competition in any market varies inversely with the height of the barriers to entry which may exist. If entry barriers are high, then the threat of potential competition insofar as it may affect the pricing policy or profit goals of the established firms is small. On the other hand, if the barriers to entry in a given market are low, then established members must "look over their shoulder" at firms not in the industry but who may enter the industry if the profit position becomes favorable.

Most important, the threat of potential competition is seen in the length of time that existing firms may be able to enjoy monopoly levels of profits. If entry barriers are small or nonexistent, the presence of above normal profit levels will act as a spur to firms in less profitable areas to enter the industry, causing a shift in the industry supply curve to the right and a reduction of market price. In an absolute monopoly nothing occurs which will tend to reduce the existing high level of profit. The height of the barrier to entry, then, is a measure of disadvantage which new sellers must overcome to achieve effective entry into a market. It is the size of the existing firms' advantage. How is this advantage to be measured? This is easier to define than it is to measure. Obviously, the best variable that may be used to define and measure the height of entry barriers is the level of transaction price charged by established sellers. More specifically, it is the difference between the level of costs facing a prospective entrant and the highest price that may be charged by existing members without attracting entry. Therefore, the height of the entry barrier varies directly with the market position of firms in the industry.

Most discussions of this aspect of industry structure divide the advantages held by existing firms into three categories: (1) those associated with the presence of scale advantages; (2) those associated with product differentiation; and (3) those associated with absolute cost advantages. The first two have already obtained our attention; it remains only to fit them into the framework of this discussion. The last category, which is least important, will be dealt with in passing. All three combine to provide the height of the entry barrier.

Product Differentiation Advantages   At this point, it should not be a surprise that product differentiation constitutes the most widespread and substantial barrier to entry, particularly in consumer goods industries. First, new entrants are seldom able to charge as high a price as established sellers upon entering an industry. Put another way, at the same price buyers prefer the products of existing producers over those of new entrants. The entrant is at a competitive disadvantage because his cost may exceed the price he can charge, or because he can only achieve a higher price by incurring promotional costs of such a magnitude that they exceed his price. Whatever the source of the disadvantage, the newcomer is faced with a substantial problem in trying to achieve a sufficient share of the market.

This second aspect of the problem is particularly important. Estimates of the cost of successfully launching a new brand of cigarettes, for example, run as high as $20,000,000 or more in advertising expenditures spread over four of five years, with no assurance of success. Studies of these expenditures in this industry indicate that advertising costs run four to five times more for new brands entering the market than for established brands. Testimony in the P & G–Clorox merger case indicate that P & G felt the entry barrier to be so high in the liquid bleach market that the only economical way that P & G could enter the market and obtain a dominant market share was through the purchase of Clorox.

Mention has also been made of the importance of the development of superior sales and service organization in entering the automobile industry. The only large-scale attempt to enter that industry, that by Kaiser-Frazer in 1946, was doomed at the outset by their inability to obtain an adequate distribution organization.[16] Faced with the fact that all of the best locations (dealerships) were in the hands of the established manufacturers they attempted to sell their cars through farm equipment dealers, used car dealers, new entrants into the industry and weaker dealers that could be attracted away from the majors. The result was disastrous for Kaiser-Frazer, proving that as long as we adhere to the current system of exclusive dealerships, new entry by domestic firms is extremely unlikely. On the other hand, Volkswagen has been fairly successful in developing precisely that type of sales organization. The basis of the popularity for the VW and most other volume sales foreign cars has been low initial price and costs of operation. Thus, new entrants are faced with overcoming existing buyer preferences, and developing a competent distribution system. In many industries these are formidable.

Scale Advantages The presence of substantial economies of scale while lowering costs may provide a substantial barrier to entry. Incoming firms, if they are to represent a viable market force, must be able to enter the market at an output level which will enable them to achieve a minimal level of scale economies, if not an optimum scale of plant. In some regional markets this may well become an important factor. The entry of new food processors into an area, for example, may be forestalled by limitations which exist with respect to the availability of raw materials. It has been alleged that one of the reasons why there has been no new entry into cement production (this does not include the acquisition of existing plants) on the West Coast is the limited availability of raw material sources. In other cases, the size of the market may simply be too small to support more than a limited number of competitors.

If scale economies of such magnitude are present, the prospective entrant must contemplate entering the industry and continuing in operation for a considerable period of time with costs substantially

---

[16] This entire period is discussed in: *Study of Administered Prices in the Automobile Industry*, Report of the Senate Subcommittee on Antitrust and Monopoly of the Committee on the Judiciary, 85th Congress, 2nd Session, Washington, D.C.: GPO, November 1, 1958, Chapters 1–4.

higher than those of established firms. Fortunately for new entrants, the presence of such scale economies are not common occurrences. The earlier discussion indicated that scale economies of a substantial magnitude exist in only a few instances. All studies in this area agree that the actual number of firms in almost all industries is smaller than would be dictated by scale economies.

Absolute Cost Advantages   Unlike the situation prevalent with respect to scale economies, where entering firms have considerable difficulties achieving a size which will enable them to avail themselves of the existing scale advantages, the presence of absolute cost advantages constitute a permanent cost advantage which is held by existing firms in the market. This type of position could be achieved as a result of superiority in production know-how, patent protection, control of raw materials or a number of other factors. Instances in which absolute cost advantages exist are relatively rare. One example where this may have occurred is in the production of steel which requires an initial investment of $100 million or more to enter the industry with an optimum size plant.

SUMMARY

The evidence with respect to changes in the level of concentration in the United States over the period since 1945 is clear. Whatever measure is selected, it has increased. In the context of this chapter it is most significant that concentration appears to have increased most in consumer good industries, while declines have occurred in producer good industries. In large measure the increases in concentration in consumer good industries could be interpreted as the result of substantial efforts of producers of these products to differentiate their products from those of their competitors. It is clear, therefore, that any discussion of the structure of markets which fails to note the importance, forms and sources of product differentiation is incomplete.

Generally, product differentiation becomes significant if it places a prospective entrant into industries at a serious disadvantage (it becomes a substantial barrier to entry), or if it simply makes it more difficult for existing firms to compete on the basis of price. On the other hand, some product differentiation in oligopoly situations may allow for considerably more price variability than is true in homogeneous oligopoly situations. This is not to say that the overall level of prices will necessarily be lower. Clearly, product differentiation affects both the competitive relationships between existing firms in an industry and between existing and potential entrants. Unless offsetting economies are realized elsewhere, it means higher costs.

The major forms of product differentiation are advertising and product development. The former is probably the most significant in terms of cost. These efforts are designed to impress the buyers with the actual or supposed differences between his product and all others of that general class. If successful, and it is obvious that much of it is, advertising encourages the development of substitution gaps between products. To the extent that these develop, competition is usually diminished.

On *a priori* grounds it would appear that the presence of differentiated products results in the elimination of some competitive pressures, that prices will be higher, and that profit levels will be in excess of those which might prevail in more open markets. This last result requires that the cost of advertising be more than offset by changes in revenue. On the other hand, consumers may feel that the *apparent* variety of products available to them may more than offset the higher costs which are associated with the high levels of product promotion necessary to develop and sustain the buyers' preferences which justify existing price differentials. However, given the general low level of consumer information, and the nature of the unequal contest between producer and consumer, it is unlikely that consumers really have any idea of the implicit choices they are making.

Not only must product differentiation be considered an important aspect of industry structure, but because of its importance it has become an important aspect of the competitive conduct of firms. Attention is given to this problem in the next chapter.

4

MARKET CONDUCT IN AMERICAN INDUSTRY

Where markets are atomistically structured, there are no opportunities for anticompetitive conduct. Firms sell as much as they want at the going price. They maximize profits by producing efficiently and by managing their production to include the most profitable combination of products. In oligopolistically structured markets, however, where concentration is relatively high and barriers to entry are significant, conduct takes on other dimensions. Firms recognize their interdependence and competitive interactions cease to be impersonal. Principal competitors are identified and reckoned with more or less individually . . . In this setting there are opportunities for anti-competitive conduct.[1]

We have looked at the major aspects of market structure at some length. All of these structural characteristics serve to condition the behavior of firms. The firm's conduct is appraised within its product market and with respect to the policies it adopts in dealing with its rivals. In perfectly competitive industries, the sole activity of the firms is the efficient production of its product. However, in imperfectly competitive markets, the conduct variables employed by firms include not only questions of efficiency of production, but such matters as pricing policy, selling expenditures and strategy, new product policy and the reactions of rivals.

As is true in competitive markets, the *bona fide* monopolist follows a standard set of rules. He simply selects that price-output combination

[1] FTC, *The Structure of Food Manufacturing, op. cit.*, p. 149.

which is optional (maximizes profit) for him. The selection of this output is made in accordance with his production and selling costs. Obviously there is some optimal size of promotion budget which yields the greatest net returns.[2] Once this is decided upon, he then makes subsequent output decisions on the basis of changes in the state of the economy—changes in demand, factor prices and technology. Since he has no rivals, the actions of others are unimportant in the selection of his price, output and promotional budget.

PRICE POLICY AND STRATEGY

Neither the monopolist nor the firm operating in a competitive industry is actively engaged in the development of a price policy. The forces of market supply and demand leave him with only one decision: How much will he produce (what is his profit-maximizing output)? To be sure, the monopolist has an option of which of the possible price-output combinations to select depending upon his preferences in terms of long run goals—profit maximization, growth maximization, sales maximization or other possible social or economic goals. However, once the firm selects a particular goal, the number of alternative price-output combinations which will enable the firm to fulfill its goal become limited, unless overall economic goals or production techniques are altered.

The firm operating in an imperfectly competitive industry is motivated by the same goals as those which hold for the monopolist. However, it faces a unique problem; its actions (price selection, output selection or entry) *may induce overt retaliatory actions by other firms* in the industry. Moreover, these overt actions on the part of other sellers, as well as by the initiating firm may result in substantial adverse effects to all firms in terms of price and profits. As some have expressed it, there is *recognized mutual interdependence* between firms. Care has been taken to suggest these effects and reactions *may* take place. Whether or not they do, and the extent to which they occur to a *greater degree than would be the case in a competitive industry* depends upon two factors: the number of firms in the industry, and the extent to which the outputs of the sellers are differentiated. Table 4-1 suggests the manner in which these two factors may interact.

Price variability in a given market is described by a set of index values scaled from zero through four. An index value of zero represents no price variability between firms in the industry, while an index value of four represents a maximum amount of variability. Irrespective of the

---

[2] While the monopolist may not engage in product promotion which is designed to distinguish his output from those of his rivals (he has none), he may attempt to influence the position and slope of the demand curve for the product.

number of sellers, it is obvious that if there is no product variation, there is price uniformity. However, as both the number of sellers and the degree of product differentiation increases, the variability in price also increases. The greater the degree of price variability in any given market, the easier price changes may be initiated by one or small groups without inducing overt retaliation by other sellers in the market. The interesting case, therefore, occurs where the price variability index takes on values between one and four.

Table 4-1   Interfirm Price Variability Index

INTERFIRM PRICE VARIABILITY	Number of Firms		
	ONE	FEW	MANY
None	0	0	0
Slight	—	1	2,3
Great	—	2,3	4

Noncollusive Pricing Behavior

When the number of sellers in an industry is small, individual firm price policy exists to some degree, even where the outputs of all sellers are identical. In such cases, however, the lag between the appearance of a price and the adjustment of other sellers to that price is quite short. Where considerable product differentiation exists, the response lag is usually increased. As the number of sellers is increased, or where the control of the leading firm is relatively small, greater price variations may exist. In such cases the lags in responding to price changes may be longer. As a result, of this lack of certainty with respect to the pricing responses of rivals in imperfectly competitive markets, a number of *possible* explanations have been developed which attempt to explain observed price behavior. Let us look first at two of the noncollusive explanations of firm pricing in oligopolistic industries.[3]

The Kinked Demand Curve—Figure 4-1   Let us assume for the moment that we are able to observe the thought processes of an executive involved in choosing a new price above or below the current price in an oligopoly situation. A whole range of possible questions could run through his mind. What will happen if I raise my price? Will other firms raise their prices if I raise my prices? If I raise my price and they do not, what will happen to my sales? What will happen if I lower my

---

[3] The explanations are advanced because they appear to correspond with observed firm behavior. They do not necessarily represent any consistent solution to a firm's pricing behavior.

price? Will other firms lower their prices if I lower my prices? If I lower my price and they do not, what will happen to my sales? We have posed two different sets of questions, with presumably different answers.

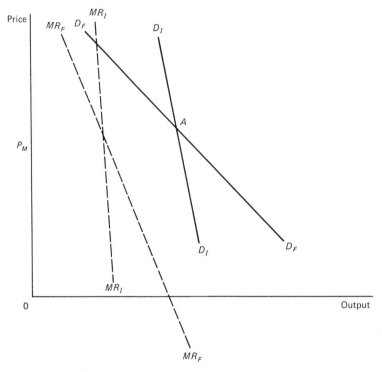

Figure 4-1   The Kinked Demand Curve

Let us look at the first set of questions. What will be the results of an increase in price by firm *A*? Let us assume that the outputs of the different sellers are similar but not perfect substitutes for each other. If firm *A* raises its price, it is obviously going to experience a reduction in sales, as long as the demand for the product is not perfectly inelastic. But, how much of a reduction in output? If firm *A* alone raises its price while the others hold theirs, it is likely that there will be a substantial shift by buyers away from its product to the product of others. Firm *A* will move up $D_F D_F$ which is substantially more price elastic than is the industry demand curve $D_I D_I$. Unless there is some underlying change in costs which affects all firms equally, firm *A* cannot logically assume that the other firms will necessarily increase their price as firm *A* does. Thus, in the situation where there is relatively little product differentiation the firm may be reluctant to initiate upward price movements for fear that it will experience a substantial reduction in its sales and profits.

What happens when firm *A* reduces its price? Again the crucial factor is the extent of product differentiation between the outputs of the different sellers. Where there is little or no product differentiation, a price reduction by firm *A* alone would mean a considerable increase in its output and revenue with any given price reduction. Depending upon its size and relative market position, the output and revenue of its rivals could be adversely effected. Given that situation, it is unlikely that *A*'s rivals will sit quietly by while firm *A* takes over a substantial part of their markets. If *A*'s rivals retaliate, the result is a general price decline with the increase in *A*'s output described by movement along AD_I rather than AD_F. The advantages which might accrue as a result of initiating a price reduction would tend to be offset by almost concurrent price reductions by its rivals, and depending upon the elasticity of demand of the industry, the net revenues of each firm in the industry may decline. Since other firms recognize this it is assumed that price will return to its previous level, P_m.

Thus, the firm in such a situation is supposedly beset with two problems: If it raises its price others will not follow; but if it lowers its price others will follow. He views the demand curve which faces him as one having a kink in it. The kink appears at the existing market price. If this logic is followed, one would presume that the market price will vary only if substantial changes occur in the supply conditions facing firms in the market. The result of adherence to this model is a high degree of price uniformity at any point in time, as well as considerable rigidity of prices through time. If the firm believes that it cannot improve its profit position by either increasing or decreasing its price, it will tend to maintain some customary price through time.

The *kinked demand curve* (see Figure 4-1) appears to provide a reasonable explanation of rational price conduct by firms in the undifferentiated oligopoly case where the number of firms is small. The fact that this explanation does not extend over a wide range of actual industry structures has led economists to seek other rational behavior models which allow for both a larger number of firms and product differentiation.

Quasicollusive Behavior

Price Leadership Models Since only a few industries exhibit the structural conditions which underly the *kinked demand curve* hypothesis, economists have sought other explanations for existing patterns of price change by firms within an industry. One such explanation suggests the existence of "price leadership." What is price leadership? How does it make itself apparent? Most simply stated, price leadership exists if firms, in response to a change in price by *one* firm in the industry, change their price in the same direction and perhaps by the same amount. Industries in which price leadership is alleged to exist are often those where recognized mutual interdependence also exists. In these industries, moreover, smaller firms feel that it is advantageous to follow the price changes initiated by the leaders. They follow the prices of larger firms up and down. One obvious effect of such behavior is a high degree of industry-wide price uniformity; however, it is not necessary that the degree of price inflexibility which exists be as high in those cases where individual firm outputs are undifferentiated. It is possible but not probable that the rigid prices will prevail in industries in which the products of various sellers are differentiated.

So far we have ignored the reasons why price leadership may prevail in an industry. Two types of basic arguments have been advanced. The first, and by far the simplest, is the so-called "dominant firm" price leadership hypothesis. This requires the existence of a firm which overwhelms all of its other rivals either in terms of sheer size or technical efficiency. In such cases, the leading firm in the industry makes its decisions with respect to product price changes on the basis of its estimate of the industry demand conditions, its cost conditions, and an estimate of the results which will prevail (particularly in terms of profit) for other members of the industry.

In such cases, the dominant firm after setting the market price must be willing to let others in the industry expand their output to meet any gap which exists between its anticipated output and total industry demand which exists at that price. Examples of such a high degree of control are difficult to find. One of the most often used examples of dominant firm price leadership is the steel industry. In the early years of the industry, U.S. Steel, because of its overwhelming size, assumed a dominant position in the industry. In retrospect, it is one of the more interesting examples of how information relating to the price and output expectations of the dominant firms was transmitted to other firms in the industry. For a brief period, the Chairman of the Board, Judge Gary, held an annual dinner to which major officials of the other steel producers were invited. The feature event of those annual meetings was a speech by the Judge. The unique feature of that speech was that moment when he would relate his views with respect to steel prices and demand for the coming year. Given the fact that U.S. Steel had 75 percent of industry capacity, it is not particularly surprising that his estimates were usually quite accurate. Under threat of antitrust prosecution, the dinners were stopped, but they remain one of the more colorful examples of an attempt by a dominant firm to coerce its rivals.

Implicit in all dominant firm price leadership arrangements is the implicit or explicit threat of the leader to take retaliatory action against firms that fail to recognize the leader's dominance. Thus, the dominant firm must stand ready to discipline rebels, either through the use of selective or general price reductions. Dominance depends exclusively upon the presence of power, and it is not necessary to show actual overt behavior by the leader to demonstrate that power is used. The clearest proof that such power exists is the fact that other firms adhere to the leader's policies without the use of that power.

A variety of names have been attached to other leadership models. However, they all have one element in common: All presume that instead of there being a dominant firm in the industry (few industries exist with truly dominant firms), a group of firms exists in an industry and that each of these firms is equipped to appraise correctly the impact upon prices of changes in the underlying supply and demand conditions which face all firms. Since any one of these firms is capable of initiating price changes in response to its appraisal of industry conditions, it would be expected that leadership would pass from one to another of these firms. The fact that other firms follow the current leader is then supposedly not a function of dominant power or even collusive action, but of mutual recognition that the price leader has interpreted correctly the changes in basic supply or demand conditions which necessitate a change in price. On occasion, firms may make abortive price changes, that others fail to follow. In these instances, the previous level of price is maintained.

This again is an example of an attempt to develop a rational, noncollusive explanation of pricing behavior in oligopolistic markets characterized by a high degree of product uniformity and mutual interdependence among sellers.

Collusive Pricing Behavior

The failure of noncollusive and quasicollusive market arrangements to provide price and profit stability in a market may be the signal for the emergence of open collusive arrangements. Noncollusive arrangements fail typically because of the lessening of the mutual interdependence felt among firms. When some firms become aware of the fact that they can get away with an independent price policy, price stability disappears. Rather than experience the rigors of open competition, firms seek methods—some legal, some illegal—of ameliorating the results of open competition. We will look briefly at some leading examples of each type.

Private Arrangements   The most spectacular method which firms have used to avoid the rigors of overt price competition has been the development of agreements between firms with respect to selling price, market territories, conditions of sale and other related aspects of behavior. These arrangements vary not only with respect to the type of con-

duct covered, but the extent to which major firms in the market participate. Arrangements vary from two participants to the industry's total
membership. Thus, some agreements are quite general while others are
limited with respect to type of conduct, geography, membership and du-
ration.

In a sense, mergers and joint subsidiaries may be the result of such an
attempt to avoid competitive pressures.[4] Here the standards are somewhat clearer regarding the legally acceptable limits of behavior. Such
agreements have been dealt with in detail elsewhere. Both the merger
and the joint subsidiary represent a somewhat more formal corporate arrangement than the usual connotations given to the term collusion.
Moreover, they may result in a somewhat different pattern of behavior
than do collusive arrangements with respect to price. Let us look briefly
at two antitrust cases which reveal interesting variations of inclusive
agreements.

One of the earliest cases in this area was unveiled in 1895.[5] The major
issue involved the competitive effects of an agreement to which all
major producers of cast iron soil pipe were parties. This was a complex
arrangement which included: (1) reserved cities in which each of the
participants had undisputed control; (2) areas in which bids were auc-
tioned off to members of the cartel on the basis of which firm would
offer the largest bribe to the other members of the cartel to get the bid;
and (3) areas in which open competition prevailed between all firms
(this coincided with the principal market area of nonagreement producers). Needless to say the members of the agreement were found guilty of
collusion and enjoined from continuing their behavior.

Since that time, a large number of price conspiracy indictments have
been filed covering dozens of different activities. Some of these involved
attempts to raise price.[6] Others were attempts to hold prices down.[7] Irrespective of the direction of the pressure on prices, the courts have
been unanimous that *all* attempts to set price or divide markets are illegal. One of the more far-reaching examples of this type of behavior
came to light in the late 1950s when the Department of Justice began
the "electrical conspiracy" cases. A Philadelphia Grand Jury investigation determined that all of the leading electrical manufacturers in the

---

[4] The joint subsidiary is a relatively recent arrangement whereby two or more
firms set up a separate corporate entity to carry on some specified business activity.
See Stanley E. Boyle, "The Joint Subsidiary: An Economic Appraisal," *The Antitrust
Bulletin*, May–June 1960, pp. 303–318; and "An Estimate of the Number and Size
Distribution of Domestic Joint Subsidiaries," *Antitrust Law and Economics Review*,
Spring 1968, pp. 81–92.

[5] Addyston Pipe and Steel *vs.* United States (1899). In its simplest form any
group of firms that cooperates formally to establish prices, allocate markets, and the
like may be called a cartel.

[6] Trenton Potteries, *et. al.* (1926).

[7] Standard Oil of Indiana, *et. al.* (1940).

country had been engaged in a gigantic conspiratorial agreement covering prices and the division of sales between cartel members of a wide variety of electrical generating and transmission equipment and stretching back, with some interruptions, for more than twenty years.

According to one investigator, "The cartel agreements were specifically designed to prevent the instigation of price competition." All sales were either open-bid or closed-bid. In open-bid sales which were conducted with large customers, the agreement was simply to maintain "list" or "book" prices. The arrangements with respect to sealed bids (which involved government agencies primarily) were quite complex, and arrived at through a lengthy series of clandestine meetings in motels, hotels, and resorts by representatives of the major producers. The effect of these meetings was the development of a system whereby sales to large users were rotated on the basis of an agreed upon percentage distribution of total sales between the conspiring companies. In each case, the lowest and highest bidders were designated in accordance with the agreement. The evidence is clear that these arrangements were imperfect. Pockets of excess capacity developed from time to time, and selective price shading would appear. In the absence of some method of disciplining recalcitrant industry members, private conspiracies can never last.

Government Sponsored Collusion   In some instances, government support provides the compulsion needed to effectuate collusive interfirm agreements. However, most government sponsored programs are somewhat more general than those referred to above and ostensibly are designed to provide some socially desirable minimum price and profit protection to struggling businesses. Fortunately, the goals of these programs have achieved almost uniformly poor results.—Success would have resulted in higher consumer prices. The best known of these include: (1) legislation forbidding sales below cost, (2) resale price maintenance legislation, (3) milk marketing agreements, (4) the entire farm support program, and in a somewhat different area (5) minimum wage legislation.

The second and third of these deserve some attention as they have succeeded to an extent which exceeds the gains usually achieved through private agreement. Also, they are of interest because if they had not been fostered by the Federal government, they would be subject to prosecution under the antitrust laws.

The basic antitrust statutes are designed to prohibit conspiracies or attempts by firms to conspire where the effect of such behavior is to set prices and allocate markets. We have seen already that private attempts to fix prices and allocate markets by firms in industry are illegal. During the 1930s, under considerable pressure from small businessmen and others, Congress passed the Miller-Tydings Act (1937) which enabled manufacturers and/or wholesalers of branded goods which are sold in open competition to establish, in cooperation with their dealers, the retail prices at which their products may be sold.[8] As a result of legislation subsequently passed (the McGuire Act) such agreements are considered to be in effect throughout a state, (for all retailers of the product) if agreement is reached between the manufacturer and/or wholesaler and one retailer within a state. Many State courts have subsequently declared these State acts to be unconstitutional, that is, the amendment runs counter to the basic provisions of the State constitution. At one time, 46 states had such statutes. Currently, only about 35 states have statutes covering non-signers.

What is the effect of such legislation? Both the intent and effect of this set of State statutes are quite clear. They allow vertical price fixing agreements between producers and retailers. The Addyston Pipe and Steel and electrical conspiracy, among others referred to above, involved price fixing by competitors in the same market, that is, horizontal price fixing, while the Fair-trade Laws allow vertical arrangements. The net effect is the same, however, uniform prices on all sales to consumers. In other words, price competition is eliminated. As you would imagine, such agreements are seldom entered into by the larger, more efficient retailers. Moreover, most large retailers have consistently refused to adhere to the prices set by such arrangements since they tend to limit their sales volume. Those retail businessmen who support this legislation are usually small, and often relatively high cost producers.

Milk marketing agreements involve the setting by State commissions of minimum retail milk prices. Firms which fail to adhere to the established prices are usually compelled, often by the courts, to set their prices in accordance with schedules established by State commissions. Again, the result is the same insofar as the consumer is concerned—uniform and *high retail* prices. These agreements are effective only because they are both sanctioned and enforced by State agencies and the courts. While producers of brand-name merchandise and small retailers have combined to support the "Fair Trade" legislation, milk marketing agreements have had considerable support from the major dairy products producers. Both have been opposed by consumer groups. In such cases, however, *consumers almost never win.*

[8] The Federal statutes do not explicitly allow resale price maintenance. Rather they grant immunity for actions by firms which are taken in accordance with the conditions of State statutes or constitutional amendments. These enabling statutes exempt firms entering such agreements from prosecution under the Clayton Act, the Federal Trade Commission Act, and the Sherman Act. These Fair Trade Acts have been consistently opposed by both antitrust agencies.

Summary

Wherever possible, firms attempt to avoid the rigors of price competition. For the most part, those not involved in overt attempts are either unable to engage in successful collusion (competitive firms), or have no competitors (monopolists). In some instances, price stability is relatively easy to achieve. This is particularly true if the number of sellers is small and the degree of product differentiation is slight. In most cases, however, agreements are not only difficult to reach, but they are difficult to maintain and are usually illegal. All *successful* long-run arrangements to set prices have one common characteristic—they are government-supported and policed. Without such support, all agreements to set prices have failed in the long run. On the other hand, some short-run agreements with respect to price have worked reasonably well.

Although the government's overall position is one supporting competition, it is unfortunate that it should use its power in any area to thrust aside the goals and results of competition. It is also a commentary on the strength of special interests in the passage of anticompetitive legislation. The effect of this type of governmental action is to raise prices to all consumers, to the benefit of some special interest group. Such a group always argues that others have managed to achieve some form of price stability as a result of some form of market imperfection, and that they should receive similar protection. These arguments assume that this is easier than and preferable to eliminating the factor (monopoly power) responsible for the maintenance of price stability in other areas. They are probably right that it is easier. The result of such action, however, is to give to all areas of the economy which are successful in achieving special interest legislation the characteristics of the more uncompetitive market structures. These arrangements also reduce the advantageous effects of profit and price changes which signal the shift of resources within the economy. As a result, price and product changes often occur too late and by too small amounts.

PRODUCT PROMOTION BEHAVIOR

There is no doubt that advertising and other product promotion activities affect the performance of industries. Sellers spend something over $18 billion annually to convince buyers of the superiority of their products over those of their rivals. The magnitude of these expenditures varies from industry to industry and from firm to firm. They are considerably more important and effective in consumer good than in producer good industries.

How do product promotion expenditures vary between industries?

What has been the trend of advertising expenditures over the past 20 years? How do advertising expenditures vary between firms of differing sizes within broad manufacturing segments and within individual industries? Which firms have the highest advertising expenditures? What changes have occurred in recent years with respect to the leading advertisers? What has been the effect of advertising expenditures upon competition?

Table 4-2   Total Advertising Expenditures: 1947–1968

Year	Advertising Expenditures[a]	Year	Advertising Expenditures[a]
1947	$ 4.3	1958	$10.3
1948	4.9	1959	11.3
1949	5.2	1960	11.9
1950	5.7	1961	11.8
1951	6.4	1962	12.4
1952	7.2	1963	13.1
1953	7.8	1964	14.2
1954	8.2	1965	15.3
1955	9.2	1966	16.7
1956	9.9	1967	16.9
1957	10.3	1968[b]	17.9

[a] Billions of dollars.
[b] Preliminary estimate.
Source: U.S. Bureau of the Census, *Statistical Abstract of the United States: 1969*, 90th ed., Washington, D.C., 1969, p. 715.

The Trend of Advertising Expenditures [9]

Advertising has become one of the more important devices open to firms in imperfectly competitive industries in promoting the sales of their products. In recent years, advertising expenditures have grown at a rapid rate. This increase has not been spread evenly throughout United States industry. Let us look first at the trend of total advertising expenditures since 1947 (Table 4-2).

Total advertising expenditures of United States corporations almost quadrupled—from $4.3 billion to $17.9 billion—between 1947 and 1968.

[9] In this, as well as other portions of this discussion, advertising will mean all product promotion expenditures. According to the Internal Revenue Service, its advertising data include "advertising identified as cost of sales or operations as well as advertising separately identified as a business deduction." Those figures tend to underestimate the actual amount for a variety of reasons including the fact that some "companies did not separately identify advertising when it was included in the cost of sales or operations." See Internal Revenue Service, *Statistics of Income—1963, Corporation Income Tax Returns*, March 1968, p. 33.

The importance of advertising appears to have increased substantially since 1962. Between 1947 and 1961, advertising expenditures increased by an average of $500 million dollars a year. Between 1962 and 1968 the average increase was more than $900 million per year—the highest rate of annual increase in advertising expenditures of the postwar period. While advertising still represents a relatively small amount of the total business receipts of all corporations, it has increased in importance. In 1966, advertising expenditures equalled slightly more than one percent of total business receipts. This represents a slight increase since 1947. While it is clear that overall advertising expenditures have increased, substantial differences exist between industries, and between firms of differing size classes within the same industry. The IRS data show generally that firm size and total advertising expenditures are positively correlated.

Advertising and Size   Advertising expenditures vary for a vast number of reasons including habit, corporate philosophy, relative position in industry, absolute size of firm, product mix, and nature of product. Of these, firm size and type of industrial activity appear to be most significant in explaining interfirm advertising variations.[10] An apparent confirmation of this can be seen from the data contained in Table 4-3.

Table 4-3   Distribution of Corporate Advertising Expenditures by Asset Size Class: 1963

Size Class [a]	Advertising Expenditures [b]	Advertising Ratios [c]
Under $1	$2.3	1.2
$1–$10	1.7	1.0
$10–$100	2.3	1.6
$100–$250	1.4	2.0
$250 & over	3.0	1.2

[a] Millions of dollars.
[b] Billions of dollars.
[c] Advertising expenditure as a percent of business receipts.
Source: U.S. Bureau of the Census, *Statistical Abstract of the United States: 1967*, 88th Ed., Washington, D.C., 1967, p. 60–61.

These data suffer from the fact that they include only corporations, thereby overestimating small firm advertising ratios. On the other hand, they include *all* corporations which may tend to bias the results obtained in any individual size class.

[10] A limited treatment of these relationships within the food manufacturing sector is contained in FTC, *The Structure of Food Manufacturing, op. cit.*, Chapter 5.

The data show, for example, that relatively small firms (those with assets of less than $1 million) do have low advertising expenditures (0.8 of one percent). Moreover, advertising ratios for other asset-size classes appear to be directly correlated with firm size. Advertising ratios of 1.0 percent prevail for firms with assets of $1 to $10 million. Corporations with assets of $100 to $250 million have advertising ratios of about 2 percent.

Firms with assets of $250 million or more, however, show advertising ratios of 1.2 percent. What explains this sudden drop? While many factors are involved, the type of industrial activity of the firms which make up this size group may be most important. In 1963, of the 692 corporations with assets of $250 million or more, more than 55 percent were engaged in finance, insurance, and real estate. Most of these were financial intermediaries (banks, savings and loan, and industrial finance companies) which have minimal advertising activities. The entire area had an advertising ratio of only 0.8 of one percent in 1963.

Despite minor variations, size of firm cannot be neglected in explaining the relative magnitude of advertising expenditures.

Distribution of Advertising Expenditures While the ratio of advertising expenditures to business receipts has increased somewhat in recent years, most of that increase has been limited to a few major industries. As you would imagine, average advertising ratios are highest in services, primarily in entertainment. They are followed quite closely by retail trade. Success in both of these areas is obviously dependent upon good consumer relations. On the other hand, such expenditures are quite low in wholesale trade. The only other major industrial sector where high advertising expenditures prevail is, of course, manufacturing. Advertising expenditure ratios do not exceed .8 of one percent in any of the other major economic sectors.

The data contained in Table 4-4 show that producers and sellers of raw materials and semifinished goods spend little money on advertising their product. First, it is not possible for them to differentiate their products from those sold by other sellers. Second, their customers are aware that the major differences which exist between the outputs of different sellers are measured in terms of the technical specifications of the product. Consequently, these buyers are seldom swayed by efforts devoted to promoting fictional characteristics of products.

Large differences exist among industry groups within the manufacturing segment (Table 4-5). In 1966, for example, advertising expenditure ratios ranged from a high of 6.1 percent for tobacco products, to a low of 0.3 percent in the production of primary metal products and transportation equipment other than motor vehicles. With rare exception, advertising ratios were relatively high for consumer good industries and low in producer good industries. The major exception, motor vehicles, has a low advertising to sales ratio because of the large dollar sales of the leading firms, not because of the low level of advertising expenditures. The advertising expenditures for the four leading car manufacturers were less than 1.5 percent of sales. On the other hand, they accounted for about 13 percent of the total advertising expenditures of the 100 largest advertisers in 1964.[11]

Table 4-4   Advertising Expenditures
by Major Industry Sectors: 1966

Industry Sector	Advertising Expenditures[a]	Advertising Ratios[b]
Agriculture, forestry and fishing	$ 28	0.3
Mining	14	0.1
Construction	120	0.2
Manufacturing	8,056	1.4
Transportation, communication and utilities	550	0.6
Retail trade	3,168	1.1
Wholesale trade	889	0.5
Finance, insurance and real estate	955	0.8
Services	747	1.8
ALL CORPORATIONS	$14,534	1.1

[a] Millions of dollars.
[b] Advertising expenditures as a percent of business receipts.
Source: Internal Revenue Service, *Statistics of Income: 1966, Corporation Income Tax Returns*, April 1970, pp. 14–27.

Here again, industry averages tend to obscure the wide variations between firms, and to underestimate the magnitude of the advertising ratios of firms in some industries. In 1966, *Advertising Age* prepared estimates of advertising expenditures to sales ratios for the 125 largest advertisers of 1964. The highest ratio appeared in the drug and medicine sector; 23 firms (approximately 20 percent of the top 125) come from this industry group. Ten drug and cosmetic producers had advertising ratios of 25 percent or more. Only three had ratios of less than 10 percent. As a group, the six soap and household cleanser producers included in the 125 largest had the second highest average level of advertising ratios; only one was under 10 percent. Cereal products, beer, gum and candy, and tobacco product producers show relatively high advertising ratios. At the other extreme, the six largest petroleum refiners had advertising ratios of 0.7 percent or lower.[12]

[11] *Advertising Age,* June 28, 1965, pp. 46–47.
[12] *Advertising Age,* January 3, 1966, p. 46.

Table 4-5   Distribution of Advertising Expenses
to Business Receipts, by Industry Group: 1966

INDUSTRY GROUP	ADVERTISING RATIO[a]
Tobacco products	6.1
Chemical products	4.2
Food and kindred products	2.4
Scientific equipment	2.5
Miscellaneous manufactures	2.2
Rubber and plastic products	1.8
Electrical machinery	1.5
Leather products	1.2
Printing and publishing	1.2
Motor vehicles and equipment	1.1
ALL MANUFACTURED PRODUCTS	1.1
Furniture	1.0
Apparel and related products	0.9
Machinery except electrical	0.8
Fabricated metal products	0.8
Paper and allied products	0.8
Stone, clay and glass products	0.8
Textile	0.6
Petroleum refining	0.6
Lumber and wood products except furniture	0.4
Primary metal products	0.3
Transportation except motor vehicles	0.3

[a] Advertising expenditures as a percent of business receipts.
Source: Bureau of Internal Revenue, *Statistics of Income: 1966,
Corporation Income Tax Returns*, April 1970, pp. 14–27.

The competitive significance of product promotion activities varies considerably with size of firm and product areas. Advertising expenditures are so large in some markets that they may become an entry barrier. At the same time, firms often advertise in the absence of significant price competition. In many of the areas we have mentioned, advertising data are available by brand through time. The cigarette industry provides an interesting example of the trend of expenditures for established brands and new brands and for major product variations (Table 4-6).

Lester Telser [13] and the Federal Trade Commission,[14] among others, have examined the timing and magnitude of cigarette advertising in total by brand. Both studies indicate that advertising and success in the

[13] Lester Telser, "Cigarettes and Advertising," *The Journal of Political Economy*, October 1962, pp. 471–499.
[14] Federal Trade Commission, *Staff Report of the Bureau of Economics on Cigarette Advertising and Output*, March 1964.

industry are positively related. The cigarette advertising data available illustrate the high cost and crucial importance of promotional expenditures in the introduction of a new brand and type of cigarette.

Table 4-6   Advertising Costs per Carton by Brand and Type of Cigarette: 1956–1964, Selected Years

		In Cents Per Carton		
BRAND	1956	1960	1962	1964
Regular				
Camel	2.5¢	2.9¢	2.8¢	3.4¢
Lucky Strike	3.0	3.0	2.6	3.7
Chesterfield [a]	3.3	4.8	7.6	7.5
Sales [b]	168.0	135.0	127.4	99.9
King				
Pall Mall	3.2	3.7	3.9	4.1
Sales [b]	57.5	68.0	72.1	70.9
Filter				
Winston	5.8	4.4	4.4	5.4
Viceroy	8.0	7.4	7.5	11.1
Tareyton	8.5	13.1	8.1	13.0
Sales [b]	65.4	83.6	92.9	107.0
Menthol				
Salem	29.4	3.7	6.9	9.9
Newport	—	17.6	14.3	19.7
Belair	—	79.5	12.3	13.9
Sales [b]	2.3	41.0	55.1	56.8

[a] Regular and king-size sales. The latter group has become increasingly important since the late 1950s.
[b] Sales of brands listed in billions of cigarettes.
Source: *Advertising Age*, January 3, 1966, p. 56.

The tremendous changes which have occurred in this industry can be illustrated by comparing sales patterns in 1952 with those of 1962. In 1952, menthol and filter cigarettes accounted for only 4.2 percent of total cigarette output and 3.7 percent of advertising expenditures. By 1962, in the face of repeated medical reports which related cigarette smoking to lung cancer and other chronic illnesses, these two types of cigarette accounted for 56.3 percent of total output and 66.1 percent of advertising expenditures.[15] This change was costly. Tables 4-6 and 4-7 show the magnitude of promotional expenditures of selected brands of cigarettes between 1956 and 1964. The dashed lines in Table 4-6 indicate years in which these brands were not sold. These data show, for example, that advertising costs for regular and king size cigarettes are relatively small,

[15] *Ibid.*, p. 38.

seldom exceeding five cents per carton. While these costs rise over the period, they do not go up by a great amount.

The proliferation of cigarette brands which followed the publication of this series of adverse medical reports has had a decided impact upon the methods and the cost of cigarette promotion. The data in Table 4-7 show, for example, the average first year promotional costs per carton of seven new brands introduced between 1959 and 1964. Per carton advertising costs of these brands ran from a low of 26.9 cents per carton to a high of $1.41 per carton. More than half exceeded 75 cents per carton. While these costs usually decline as sales rise, they remain high years after the introduction of a new brand. Filter cigarette advertising costs are three times larger than those of regular cigarettes, while the advertising costs of menthol cigarettes average approximately twice those of filter cigarettes.

Table 4-7   First Year Advertising Expenditures

Brand	First Year	Advertising Costs Per Carton[a]	1964 Sales[b]
Lark	1963	84.4	9.4
Belair	1960	79.5	6.1
Alpine	1959	45.7	2.8
Paxton	1963	26.9	2.3
Montclair	1963	105.0	2.0
Spring	1964	38.6	1.7
Tempo	1964	141.0	1.5

[a] Cents per carton.
[b] Billions of cigarettes.
Source: *Advertising Age*, January 3, 1966, p. 56.

Conditions in the cigarette industry, as evidenced by these data, suggest that the structure of the industry has had significant effect on the conduct of firms; uniform conduct reactions are easier to specify and achieve when markets include three, four or five large firms. The competitive emphasis of the conduct of these firms has been transferred from the area of price competition to that of product promotion competition. The level of these expenditures has been quite high in the years immediately following the introduction of a new brand. In recent years, expenditures on a single brand have run as high as $10,000,000 per year. Over the postwar period, this has become an increasingly important aspect of the competitive conduct of firms in this industry. In 1946, for example, cigarette advertising expenditures equalled about 2.1 percent of business receipts; by 1964 this figure had increased to approximately 6.1 percent. This represents not only a basic change in the conduct of cigarette manufacturers, but is indicative of the extent to which they have gone in attempting to influence smoking habits of consumers in the face of the overwhelming medical evidence relating early death to cigarette smoking.

It is clear that any firm contemplating entry into the industry, or any existing firms seeking to introduce a new brand, seek to attract new customers, not by means of price competition, but through cigarette advertising.

SUMMARY

We have not attempted to provide a detailed critique of the various effects of different modes of firm conduct. We have examined some explanations of firm behavior which seem consistent with imperfectly competitive structural models. It is not surprising, therefore, that the forms of conduct evidenced by firms in such industrial structures are not consistent with those suggested for competitive firms. We have shown, moreover, that in many imperfectly competitive situations emphasis shifts from product pricing to various aspects of product promotion. In some cases this represents actual changes in the nature of the product; in others it is a simple appeal to supposed qualities which the products are assumed to have.

It does not matter to economists, however, whether or not the products are actually different in physical or chemical characteristics. If consumers feel that there are differences and express these preferences (pay more for one product over another *or* buy substantially greater amounts of one product at the same price) then imperfections exist in the market. Unfortunately, the available evidence (which is admittedly limited) shows also that the less informed, the less educated, the less sophisticated the buyer is, the more likely it is that sellers will be able to induce substitutions between products. On the other hand, larger, more informed, educated and sophisticated industrial consumers succeed in eliminating these supposed differences and purchase the same products primarily on the basis of physical or chemical specifications and quality.

In many industries, and for many products, product promotion expenses assume substantial proportions. Leading firms in some consumer good industries allocate sums equal to more than 25 percent of total their sales for advertising and general sales promotion. Many consumers and consumer organizations question the value of activities whose basic purpose seems to be the raising of price. Is this evidence of economic waste? Does this activity achieve some useful end in the society? In many areas advertising and promotion expenditures are of such a magnitude as to result in significant increases in costs of distribution and ultimately in price. Clearly, they represent a significant form of behavior which may effect the tone and intensity of interfirm competition.

5

MARKET PERFORMANCE

Preceding chapters examined some of the more important characteristics of basic market structure. That examination focused on such variables as the number and relative size of firms, industry and company growth, the height of entry barriers and the like. The conduct of firms in industries has been examined also. Here the emphasis was upon the nature of promotional activities undertaken, price and product decisions, the presence and/or absence of collusion and related activities. Our interest in these variables is twofold. First, we are interested in their incidence. Second, and more important, we are interested in the way in which changes in them are reflected in the performance of the market.

How does one measure the performance of an industry? Ideally, we are interested in determining the extent to which the structure of the industry and the conduct of its members may have desirable or undesirable effects upon distribution of income and allocation of goods and services between competing uses. On the surface the measurement of these effects may seem deceptively simple.

Here as in other areas, data limitations have forced researchers to resort to indirect quantitative measures of the efficiency of the allocative process. These measures attempt to relate efficiency, to specific characteristics of market structure, usually the level of concentration. Unfortunately, these relationships must be considered as only rough measures of the performance of markets. This examination will forego any treatment of aspects of market performance which are not capable of quantitative treatment. As a consequence, it does not include an appraisal of the pro-gressiveness of markets. This is true despite the fact that the speed with which a market develops and introduces new processes and production techniques is a matter of considerable interest.

On *a priori* grounds, economic theory assumes that competitive firms will introduce cost-saving innovations as rapidly as possible in the hope that they will gain a temporary advantage over their rivals. In other words, their basic competitive weapon is efficiency (lower costs). Some assume that without the prod of competition, the pace of technological progress would be slow. Moreover, they hold that its speed is deter-mined not by the pace of innovation but by considerations relating to the maintenance of orderly markets and long-run inter-firm relations, as well as a desire to avoid outbreaks of open price competition. It is not clear, however, whether or not it is possible to distinguish or measure these pressures with certainty or precision. Moreover, assuming that firms follow some form of maximizing behavior, it is not clear that firms in imperfectly competitive industries, in fact, behave much differently from those in competitive industries.

This variable is excluded from examination here for yet another rea-son. Unambiguous measures of the speed of technological progress are impossible to derive unless one is willing to count patents, to measure the number and cost of pieces of capital equipment and the like. Given these limitations, measuring differences in the rate of technological inno-vation associated with differences in the structure of an industry is a highly complex problem, beyond the scope of this book.

Our attention here is devoted to the measurement of industry perfor-mance in three general areas. First, the efficiency of a market can be ap-praised through an examination of price-cost differentials in both the short and long run. These relationships are reflected in the size of firm profit rates or profit margins in specific markets through time and be-tween industries at any point in time, that is, in the relationship be-tween profitability and concentration. A second measure of the perfor-mance of industries that will be examined is the relationship between the level of wages and the level of concentration. In other words, do mo-nopolists (or firms with substantial monopoly power) exert their power and force workers to take lower than competitive wages, or are domi-nant firms less cost conscious than firms in more competitive industries, and therefore allow higher than competitive wages? The third aspect of performance to obtain our attention is the relationship between levels of concentration and advertising expenditures.

These do not exhaust the possible areas of examination. They do, however, represent activities about which data of a reasonably high quality are available. More important, these data enable the student to obtain a picture of both the measures suggested and the analytical techniques employed by economists in appraising the performance of markets.

MEASURES OF PERFORMANCE

The prospect of profits, or fear of losses, translates the forces of supply and demand into operating decisions of firms. As firms respond, competitive firms adjust profit levels toward the *cost* of capital. Departures for extended periods of time of industry profit levels from the cost of capital reflects weaknesses and probable imperfections in the forces bringing about their adjustment. Prolonged high profits usually indicate a lack of rigorous competition among established firms and impeded entry of new firms. *The general level of profits in an industry is thus a useful index of overall performance and an indicator of the vigor of competition.*[1]

Attempts to analyze the performance of competition through the measurement of profits, cost-profit margins, gross margins, or some related measure have been underway since the early 1930s. While many useful insights were gained from some of these early studies, the first study which related industry performance to industry structure in a systematic manner appeared in 1951.[2] Since then, many studies have appeared which purport to measure either (1) the direction and causes of changes in profit levels *through time*, or (2) the degree to which a direct relationship exists between profit rates and concentration levels at some point in time. Some of these studies are cross-sectional, others attempt to relate changes in the structure-performance relationship through time. While some differences of opinion exist, the majority of these studies conclude that a significant positive relationship exists between the level of concentration and profitability.

Concepts and Problems

Profits Defined   At this point it is useful to review some of the differences which exist between the concept of economic profits and profits as they are traditionally measured in an accounting sense. In large part, the differences between economic and accounting profits stem from the basic differences in defining costs.

Accounting profit data are generally available for the firm or, if all the firms producing a given set of competing products are included, for the

[1] Federal Trade Commission, *The Structure of Food Manufacturing, op. cit.*, p. 181. Emphasis added in last sentence.
[2] Joe S. Bain, "Relation of Profit Rate to Industry Concentration," *Quarterly Journal of Economics*, August 1951, pp. 293–324.

industry. Accounting profit (P_A) is defined as total revenue (R_t) minus total current costs (C_c) (cost of materials, labor, electricity, water, distribution and the like), minus current changes for past costs (C_p) (depreciation, depletion and the like). In this manner accounting or book profit is simply: $R_t - C_c - C_p = P_A$. Such figures are usually available from financial statements for the corporation and in a limited number of instances for its major subdivisions. However, it is rare to find such data available for the production of individual products or for that matter for whole product lines. "Rate of profit" is measured as accounting book profit as a percentage of owners' investment (equity), sales, total assets or some other variable used as a base. Owners' equity is the most widely accepted base and is probably more appropriate than others for the measurement of the flow of capital in the market among alternative uses.

Inadequate as the data are, firms use them for purposes of comparing their performance in some period with that of past periods. If sufficiently detailed, the firm will probably use these estimates to compare the performance of one product line, plant or division against others. In this way they are able to assess the overall contribution of a product line, plant or subsidiary to the financial well-being of the company. Finally, such data are used to compare the performance of the company with that of other companies. Such comparisons are made within the firm and by investors in the market. It should be remembered, however, these data are at best rough measures of corporate profitability.

As profits are defined in an economic sense, they involve another factor: the costs which the company incurs as a result of the fact that its funds are invested in this particular activity rather than being invested somewhere else. Economic profit, therefore, must be computed after an allowance is made for the cost of foregone opportunities. Thus, economic profits (P_0) are equal to total revenue (R_t) − current costs (C_c) − past costs (C_p) − opportunity costs (C_o). Unless we arrive at that unlikely situation where capital is costless (a zero interest rate) or where the rate of return in all activities is the same, accounting profit (P_A) must always be higher than economic profit (P_E). Thus, accounting profits usually overstate the actual level of economic profits in the industry. Moreover, while firms may make *accounting profits* they may at the same time experience *economic losses;* for instance, they might make more if they invested their money in some other venture of comparable risk.

A brief look at the determinants of the level of opportunity costs will be useful before continuing with this discussion of profits. Most of the specific factors which determine the magnitude of opportunity costs can be described by one word—risk. Risk exists in many forms. For example, a product or service might or might not sell. If it is a new product, the risk associated with investment in its production might be quite high. If it is a slight variation of a currently successful product, the risk might be low. The extent of competition in a particular industry might also be thought of as an investment risk.[3] If firms are able to protect their technological advances for only a brief period of time, then such investments might have to be recovered in a relatively short period of time to make them economically feasible for the company. The capability of the firm's management is an additional element of risk from the point of view of the potential investor. Thus, *ceteris paribus* the more competent the management of the corporation, the less risk assigned to any specific action by it. This variable may outweigh all other effects in many instances.

A variety of specific points might be added to the three factors mentioned above. In large measure, however, they would duplicate those mentioned. The point to be kept in mind is that the level of opportunity costs may vary between firms, between industries, and in some cases, between product lines. There is no single level of opportunity costs which applies to all areas of economic activity and which, when subtracted from accounting profits, gives the economic profit (or loss) in a particular market. It is important to keep this point in mind in evaluating the performance of United States industry since most analyses of industry profit differentials are based on accounting profits. Assuming for the moment that all firms in any area under examination use comparable accounting systems, there is no reason to assume that *all* resulting differences in profit actual levels should be attacked as manifestations of economic power. In other words, if the rate of return is 8 percent in the production of wheels and 10 percent in the production of blocks, there is no *a priori* basis for concluding that block manufacturers are making excess profits (assuming that an accounting rate of return of 8 percent is at least an equitable economic rate of return for the manufacture of wheels). What might be expected in competitive markets *in the long run* is that the relationship between actual rates of return and opportunity costs will be proportional to levels of risk.

Profits Measured   The Appendix to Chapter 1 contains some suggestions of sources which might be utilized in developing firm and industry profit data. Unfortunately, these sources provide information relating to only the level of accounting profits. The data available from these sources were developed by firms for tax purposes, internal management control or for showing stockholders the current profits (or

---

[3] Many firms have joined in joint ventures for the ostensible purpose of reducing the magnitude of this risk for individual companies. See S. E. Boyle, "The Joint Subsidiary: An Economic Appraisal," *The Antitrust Bulletin*, May–June 1960, pp. 303–318; and W. J. Mead, "The Competitive Significance of Joint Ventures," *The Antitrust Bulletin*, Fall 1967, pp. 819–849.

losses) or growth experienced by the firm compared with some preceding period. Therefore, the economist who attempts to use them to measure inter-industry profit differentials encounters substantial problems.
Data necessary to the development of accurate estimates of economic
profits are seldom, if ever, available. Consequently, minor differences (or
small changes) in profit levels should not be interpreted as necessarily
representative of anything.

The unavailability of product or divisional cost and profit data com-
pounds the problem. As the large corporation has assumed increased importance and has become more and more diversified, corporate profit
data relate less to any single area of operation and are more the result
of a package of diversified interests. As long as firms were basically sin-
gle-product, single-plant firms, summary corporation cost and profit data
may have been usable and sufficient to analyze the operation of markets.
The usefulness of these data diminishes rapidly, however, where firms
are engaged in the production of different products, in different sectors
of the economy. The analysis of performance must then be undertaken
through the use of a number of proxy variables of uneven quality. Like
politics, industrial organization and often all of economics becomes the
art of the possible.

In recent years, considerable pressure has developed to require divisional, or even more refined, accounting information.[4] These efforts are
largely the result of the inability of economic and investment analysis to
provide meaningful explanations of firm behavior on the basis of the
partial and sometimes misleading data currently available to investors
and regulatory agencies. Due to the overwhelming opposition of business firms, there is some doubt that these efforts will meet with much
success in the near future, however desirable such changes might seem
to some.

Accounting profit data are available for listed corporations from annual company reports and general financial manuals. Similar data are
available for broad industry categories.[5] The usual process employed in
compiling these industry totals is to place the data for each company
into that industry which accounts for the largest (but not necessarily the
major) share of its total sales. Given the diversity of firm activity, profit
data for such broad categories obviously hide a multitude of product-
mix variations among the firms classified in each industry group. The
usual published data do not provide any easy way of determining the

⁴ *Economic Concentration: Concentration and Divisional Reporting, Part 5,* Hearings before the Senate Subcommittee on Antitrust and Monopoly of the Committee
on the Judiciary, 1967.
⁵ These data are collected and appear in reports of the Internal Revenue Service
and in the *Quarterly Financial Report,* a joint publication of the Federal Trade
Commission and the Securities and Exchange Commission.

importance of the firm in the industry or how important any given industry is to any firm. Thus, it is difficult, if not impossible, to determine the precise source of a firm's sales and profits.

This does not mean that such data have no value. It does mean, however, that considerable care must be taken in the use of company data and in any interpretation which is made of the results obtained using the data.

Studies of Firm Profitability   Many of the early studies of profit differentials between firms and/or industries were aimed at either (1) explaining differences in rates of returns earned by companies engaged in the manufacture of the same products, that is, differences in efficiency, or (2) appraising the premerger and postmerger profit positions of firms which had engaged in significant merger activity.

Typically, such studies showed that most of the larger companies earned higher rates of return than did smaller ones. These differences were often explained as being the result of the greater efficiency of the larger firms compared with the smaller firms. While such an explanation has some charm on the surface, it ignores the entire question of the relative economic power of large and small firms.

Large firms, due to their significant buying power, may be able to squeeze cost concessions out of *smaller, less powerful suppliers* beyond those which are based upon actual differences in the cost of serving the larger customer. Given that these lower prices may not be available to their smaller competitors, the lower costs and higher profits may simply represent a transfer of money from the smaller supplier to the larger buyer with *no net social gain.* However, there are many obvious reasons why firms might grant price concessions to large buyers which are not related solely to the bargaining power of the buyer. Thus, while these transfers may not result in any social gains neither do they necessarily result in any social losses. Considerations of equity aside, it is clear that profit differences between firms of varying sizes cannot be attributed necessarily to efficiency without the introduction of other variables which take into account variations in size or economic power itself.

Merger Growth and Profitability   Economists and others have been interested in the causes and effects of merger activity. It is not surprising, therefore, that many of the earlier studies of the relationship between corporate size and profitability came about as a result of the efforts of researchers to demonstrate that merger activity either resulted in improved economic results, or perhaps more commonly that the reverse was true. Therefore, it is somewhat ironic that many of the early studies of the success of merger activity showed that the combined (postmerger) firms earned rates of return which were lower than the individual companies had immediately prior to merger. Both Dewing and Livermore concluded that many, if not most, of the significant mergers they analyzed were unsuccessful if measured by comparing premerger and postmerger profit rates.[6]

Recent tests of merger success based on profitability are contained in somewhat complementary studies by Reid and Hogarty.[7] Reid's study, which compares the growth and profit experience of actively merging and nonmerging firms, showed that companies which engaged in considerable merger activity typically showed *lower rates of return* than did firms which engaged in little or no merger activity. This study shows, moreover, that "success" is a relative thing and that depending upon how it is measured (increased sales, growth in assets, or some other measure), markedly different conclusions can be reached. For example, despite the fact that those firms which actively engaged in mergers had lower profit rates they exhibited considerable faster rates of growth in assets than nonmerging companies.

Hogarty's study represents in part a modern test of the classic premerger versus postmerger profit comparisons. His results which are based on a relatively small sample of 43 merging companies, shows that only a few of the large mergers consummated in the past few years could be considered successful. In fact, his results seem to show a lower rate of success during the 1950s and 1960s than those shown by either Livermore or Dewing for the 1920s and 1930s.

The earlier studies by Livermore and Dewing and the recent ones by Reid and Hogarty all deal with the relationship between the firm's profitability and its size. While this is an interesting and highly useful type of analysis, *it does not bear directly* upon the question of the relationship between monopoly power and market performance. Once again it may confuse the substantial differences between monopoly power and absolute size.

---

[6] A. S. Dewing, "A Statistical Test of the Success of Consolidations," *Quarterly Journal of Economics*, November 1921, pp. 84–101; and, Shaw Livermore, "The Success of Industrial Mergers," *Quarterly Journal of Economics*, November 1935, pp. 69–96.

[7] Samuel Richardson Reid, "Corporate Mergers and Acquisitions Involving Firms in Missouri: Some Economic Results and Administrative Policies and Processes," unpublished dissertation, St. Louis University, 1962; and Thomas J. Hogarty, "The Measurement and Analysis of Success in Corporate Mergers," unpublished dissertation, State University of New York at Buffalo, 1969. A brief description of Reid's study is contained in his *Mergers, Managers and the Economy*, New York, McGraw-Hill Book Company, Inc. 1968, Chapter 2. A recent study of the premerger growth and profitability characteristics of large corporations acquired showed that they typically grew faster and were more profitable that the average firms of their size and in their industry classification. Stanley E. Boyle, "Pre-Merger Growth and Profit Characteristics of Large Conglomerate Mergers in the United States: 1948–1968," *St. John's Law Review*, Spring 1970, pp. 152–170.

Testing Performance   Some of the limitations which exist with respect to the quality of the data available for testing structure-performance relationships have already been discussed. The appropriateness of the variables representing the changes has been examined also. Despite the problems involved, they are probably the best available for our purpose. The problem is then to select an analytical method which will enable us to obtain accurate and meaningful quantitative measures of the relationship between these variables. Like most studies we will select some measure of concentration as the structure variable and rate of profit for the performance variable. The question we hope to answer is: Do profit rates increase as the degree of monopoly (concentration) increases? The method usually employed in such two-variable analyses is the simple "least squares" regression or correlation technique. Many of you are familiar with the technique and excellent discussions can be found in almost any statistics book. Our purpose here is much more limited—to explain what the results so obtained mean.[8] This type of analysis answers one question: How much of the one observed variation can be explained by changes in another variable? To what extent are movements in the two variables correlated? The three examples in Figure 5-1 show the extreme ranges possible.

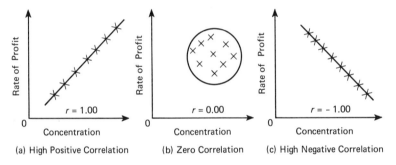

(a) High Positive Correlation   (b) Zero Correlation   (c) High Negative Correlation

Figure 5-1   Visual and Numerical Correlation Values

Figure 5-1(a) shows a direct and positive, in fact, a perfect relationship between our two variables (rate of profit and concentration). The rate of profit rises proportionately as concentration increases. A line which connects all of the profit-concentration coordinates for each industry (hypothetical observations shown by an X) is best described as a straight line. This gives a simple correlation coefficient, r, equal to 1.00 between the variables. This represents a perfect fit—the sum of the squared deviations from this line equals zero. In this instance, *all* changes in the rate of profit *appear* to be explained by changes in the level of concentration.

[8] My thanks to my colleague Frank Falero who suggested that this type of simple approach be used to explain the use of the results of simple correlation analysis.

Figure 5-1(c) is arranged in such a way that the two variables are related inversely. As concentration increases, rate of profit declines. Here again all of the observations fall on a straight line. In this case, however, there is a perfect inverse relationship with $r = -1.00$. Again all changes in the rate of profit *appear* to be a direct result of a change in the level of concentration. It should be pointed out that the direction of causation has been hypothesized to run from structure to performance. The data would support the opposite hypothesis equally well.

Figure 5-1(b) is an illustration showing the opposite extreme. An analysis of the movements of the two variables shows them to have absolutely no consistent pattern. Put another way, there *appears* to be no way in which changes in the level of concentration affect the rate of profit. In such cases, $r = 0.00$.

Simple logic would suggest that the true relationship between any pair of economic variables is seldom at either extreme. Most actual cases fall somewhere between the two extremes because: (1) changes in one variable are almost never complete and perfect explanations of changes in another (some come very close but are not perfect), and (2) at the other extreme, it is unlikely that two variables which seem to be related logically will show zero correlation.[9] Even under adverse conditions, changes in one variable *appear* to explain changes in another, even though the degree of explanation may be small.

Let us look at a simple hypothetical example using concentration and rate of return as our two variables and see what tentative conclusions can be drawn regarding their relationship. Each X in Figure 5-2 represents a particular rate of profit and level of concentration in an industry. The scatter shown depicts that relationship in ten industries. Our question is again to what extent changes in the level of concentration appear to explain changes in the rate of profit. Assuming the values shown in Figure 5-2, a value for $r = .80$ is obtained. This is generally considered to show "strong" correlation between the variables. The value obtained for r^2, which is called the coefficient of determination, measures the amount of the total variation in rate of profit that is explained by changes in concentration. In this example $r^2 = 0.64$. Thus in this example almost two-thirds of the total change in rate of profit is explained by changes in

[9] It is possible to obtain relatively high correlation values between variables which would not appear to be causally related. For example, we might get a large but inverse correlation between milk as a percentage of total food diet, and the number of teeth in one's mouth. If this result were accepted uncritically one might obtain some interesting conclusions: (1) high rate of milk consumption adversely affects the development of teeth, or (2) people with teeth can't drink milk. In this particular example the high value of the correlation coefficient between these two variables is a function of the fact they are both due to some third factor—the age of the person. Infants drink milk; infants don't have teeth or digestive systems which allow them to consume food. If variables do not appear to be related in any logical way then the analysis should stop.

concentration *alone*. One question remains: Since it is always possible that some set of random events will give a good result, we must find out what the likelihood is that the result obtained could have been a random event. How much confidence do we have in the estimate? This is a relatively simple task. Reference to an appropriate set of tables indicates that the result we obtained in our hypothetical example could have occurred by *chance* in a maximum of 1 out of 100 cases. We would then say that the relationship between the two variables was significant at the 99 percent level, and we could feel fairly safe in using and interpreting the results that are obtained.

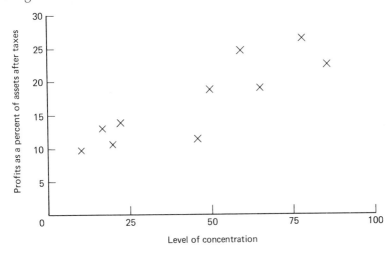

Figure 5-2   Profits and Concentration

Much of the remainder of this chapter makes use of this rather simple form of statistical analysis. It is hoped that this brief explanation will assist in making the studies referred to more meaningful.

Monopoly Power and Profitability   A number of studies have dealt directly with the relationship between concentration and profitability. Again assuming that concentration is an acceptable proxy for monopoly power, these studies attempt to relate the degree of concentration in an industry to the rate of profit at some point in time or over time. The first of these studies appeared in 1951 and was made by Bain.[10]

The Bain study covers 42 of the 340 manufacturing industries defined by the Bureau of the Census in 1935. It is restricted to those which are nationwide markets and those in which there is a high degree of specialization, that is the firms in the industry primarily produce products clas-

[10] Joe S. Bain, "Relation of Profit Rate to Industry Concentration: American Manufacturing, 1936–1940," *op. cit.*

sified in the industry; this reduces the diversification problems mentioned earlier. In total, Bain used profit data for some 333 firms in his analysis.[11] The data were compiled by the Securities and Exchange Commission and the variable used was "profits after taxes on net worth." To reduce the effect of random fluctuations, the profit rates of the firms were averaged over the five-year period.

The profit rates obtained were then compared to the appropriate eight-firm industry concentration ratio, using value of output as measured in 1935. Bain concluded, "A regression line fitted to the data shows a decided downward slope for profit ratio as concentration decreases, but the correlation is poor $(r=.33)$. . . . The general showing is that of a fairly high level of profit rates down to the 70 percent concentration line. . . . There is a significant difference in the average of industry average profit rates above and below this line . . ."[12] Subsequent reexamination of these basic data by Collins and Preston reveals a slightly lower correlation $(r=.28)$. However, they conclude that the profit differences above and below the 70 percent concentration ratio are significant at the 98 percent level.[13] Thus, while the correlation coefficient was not high, it was significant. One of the most recent cross-section studies shows roughly the same result. In an analysis of the relationship between concentration and "profit margins" in all 417 census industries for 1963, Collins and Preston obtain r^2 values between the variables of .10.[14] Thus, while Bain was unable to demonstrate the presence of a continuous relationship between concentration and profitability, he did demonstrate that firms in more highly concentrated industries appear to enjoy higher levels of profits than those in less concentrated industries.

In subsequent years, a variety of studies by Fuchs, Weiss, Levinson, Schwartzman, Stigler, Sheppard, Kamerschen, Miller and Collins and Preston, among others, have tended to substantiate Bain's original conclusion.

The studies referred to above analyze the association between the two variables as if it were a simple linear relationship. An interesting exception to this approach is contained in two studies by the Federal Trade Commission.[15] The first of these studies tested "the hypothesis that a

[11] The firms included both large and small companies. Measured in terms of net worth, 55 firms were in the $50 million and over size class, 78 had assets between $10 and $50 million, 149 between $1 and $10 million, and 51 had a net worth of less than $1 million. *Ibid.*, p. 320.

[12] *Ibid.*, pp. 313–314.

[13] N. R. Collins and Lee Preston, *Concentration and Price-Cost Margins in Manufacturing Industries*, Berkeley, Cal., University of California Press, 1968, p. 23.

[14] N. R. Collins and Lee Preston, "Industry Structure and Profitability," paper prepared for the Western Economic Association, August 1968, p. 5.

[15] Federal Trade Commission, *The Structure of Food Manufacturing, op. cit.*, pp. 202–210, and *Economic Report on the Influence of Market Structure on the Profit Performance of Food Manufacturing Companies*, 1969.

firm's profit is determined by the structure of the industry (or industries) which it occupies."[16] It shows also the gains available from the use of detailed individual firm data in the analysis of the relationship between profits and market position.

Using data collected by the Commission in an earlier study, a unique weighted index of individual firm concentration for 1950 was constructed.[17] The data used showed the share held by each of 85 of the largest food manufacturers in each of its industries, as well as the importance of each of those industries to the total sales of each company. These, when combined with industry concentration data, made it possible to construct individual company concentration indexes. These weighted concentration indexes depicted numerically the composite position of each company in each of the industries in which it was a producer.[18] These weighted company concentration indexes were then related to the company profit position (Table 5-1).

Table 5-1 Company Concentration Ratios
and Profit Rates: 1950

COMPANY CONCENTRATION RATIO	NUMBER OF COMPANIES	WEIGHTED PROFIT RATE[a]
(percent)		(percent)
30–39	21	6.2
40–49	32	9.2
50–59	15	12.9
60–69	6	14.6
70–79	11	16.3

[a] Net profit after taxes as a percent of net worth.
Source: FTC, *Report on Food Manufacturing*, 1966, p. 206.

The companies were then grouped by concentration ratio and level of concentration and profit rates were correlated. The results showed two interesting relationships. First, the relationship between the two variables may be non-linear (line A, Figure 5-3). An analysis of the data indicates that a quadratic equation fits the data slightly better than if a single linear relationship between the two variables is assumed (line B,

[16] *The Structure of Food Manufacturing, op. cit.,* p. 203.
[17] *Report of the FTC on Industrial Concentration and Product Diversification in the 1000 Largest Manfacturing Companies,* 1957.
[18] The method employed reduces the influence of random changes in profit position. In addition, the effect of firm size is reduced as much as possible. For example, a very large company with a relatively small share of each of the markets it occupies would have a very low concentration index, particularly if the level of concentration was low in each. On the other hand, a relatively small firm with a large share of highly concentrated industry would have a high index. The 1969 study uses a somewhat more complex approach but deals basically with the same question.

Figure 5-3). Second, the correlation coefficients obtained using this method of analysis were substantially higher than those shown in any other studies: linear; $r^2 = .81$, quadratic, $r^2 = .83$. While a part of this may be due to the grouping methods employed, a more substantial portion derives from their ability to construct a concentration index which more accurately represents the positions of the leading firms.[19]

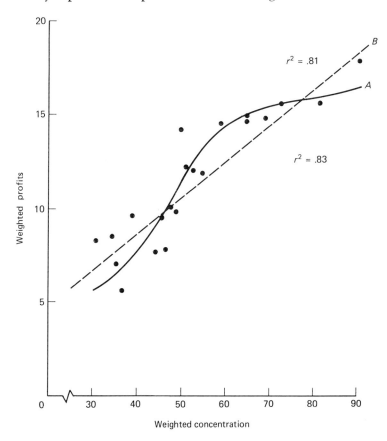

Figure 5-3   Weighted Concentration and Profit Rates for 85 Food Manufacturers: 1950

The near unanimity of most of the studies in this area should not lead the reader to the conclusion that the subject is closed or that there remain no problems to be solved. To repeat an earlier observation, most studies show the relationship between concentration and profitability to be significant but small. However, in almost all of these, the minor magnitudes involved suggest that either other factors account for relative

[19] FTC, *The Structure of Food Manufacturing, op. cit.*, pp. 202–210.

profit levels or the variables used thus far have been improperly defined. There is some reason to believe that the latter alternative is more important. A few studies, including those by the FTC and another by Hall and Weiss,[20] report substantially higher values than those which were obtained previously. A careful examination of these studies shows that they used rather well-defined product and company data. In other words, the results obtained in simple 4-digit industry cross-section studies are seriously affected by a variety of random factors. As a consequence, it is not possible to obtain unambiguous results. Moreover, it is clear that considerable effort might be spent in improving the quality of the available data or in the development of better and more sensitive methods of measuring industry differentials.

Although the problem is mentioned above (pages 103–105) it is well to point out that a major portion of the problem of low correlation values between these two variables may arise from the present limitations on the availability of an appropriate measure of profitability. Actual profit data are available from the Internal Revenue Service *Source Book* on the equivalent of a 3-digit industry group basis. Unfortunately, the concentration data available at this level of aggregation are fragmentary and of uneven quality. On the other hand, rather good concentration data are available on a 4-digit (industry) and 5-digit (product class) basis but no profit data.[21]

In an effort to overcome this problem, a number of economists have attempted to force the concentration data which are available at the four-digit industry level (usually at the 4- or 8-firm level) into 2- and 3-digit industry groups. These "average" concentration values are assumed then to be sufficiently comparable to the profit data which are available at that level to facilitate meaningful structure-performance analysis. Since the profit data cannot be disaggregated, the reverse process is not possible.

The average concentration rate is constructed by weighting each four-digit industry concentration ratio by its total value of shipments, and then correlating it with the appropriate profit rate.[22] If the average

[20] Marshall Hall and Leonard Weiss, "Firm Size and Profitability," *Review of Economics and Statistics,* August 1967, pp. 319–331.

[21] Those using Census data usually use a profit margin which represents value added—payroll (wage and salary payments to employees) over total value of shipments. The magnitude of this fraction of course may vary from industry to industry for reasons other than firm size and degree of monopoly power. At the present time, little is known of the relationship between this variable and profits.

[22] For recent examples of this method see R. W. Kilpatrick, "The Choice Among Alternative Measures of Industrial Concentration," *Review of Economics and Statistics,* May 1967, pp. 258–260; R. W. Kilpatrick, "Stigler on the Relationship Between Industry Profit Rates and Market Concentration," *The Journal of Political Economy,* May/June 1968, pp. 479–488; and R. A. Miller, "Marginal Concentration Ratios and Industrial Profit Rates: Some Empirical Results of Oligopoly Behavior," *The Southern Economic Journal,* October 1967, pp. 259–266.

concentration ratio is to serve as a usable estimate of actual levels of concentration, at least two conditions should be met. First, the four or eight largest firms in an industry must occupy a similar position in *each other* industry, if they are to actually be included among the leading firms in the largest universe for which a concentration estimate is sought. Second, the same universe (the same firms) should be encompassed by both data sets. For example, one can hardly expect a high degree of success if Census of Manufactures "value of shipments" concentration data are used to explain profit levels computed from IRS data, unless the same firms are included for each industry group in the separate data sets.[23]

In many 4-digit industries the proportion of firms likely to be excluded in the preparation of average concentration ratios may well be somewhat larger. In each case, the representativeness of the weighted index depends upon the degree of diversification of the companies represented among the leaders in each of the industry groups.[24] In an effort to determine the likelihood of the accuracy of the average concentration ratio, a simple simulation model was developed to deal with one of the least complex cases possible. That paper assumed a single three-digit industry group with three 4-digit industry subclasses each with eight different firms (a total of 24 firms). The conclusion reached there was that the ideal situation was likely "to occur only 1 time out of 4900. Since this example is far less complex than any which occur in the real world, it seems clear that the *necessary* and *sufficient* condition for the weighted coverage to equal the actual concentration . . . would almost never be satisfied."[25]

The studies referred to above show that the simple aggregation approach can be employed only if the actual distribution of firm approximates the theoretical minimum. It is clear that the greater the divergence between the actual and theoretical minimum curves, the greater the error involved in using the average concentration index as a measure of concentration. The data shown in Figure 5-4 indicate that the error involved in the use of such an average index may be substantial. In addition, other tests using data for 1950 and 1963 show that the average figures are always greater than the actual level of concentration.

---

[23] FTC, *The Structure of Food Manufacturing, op. cit.,* p. 238.

[24] For extensive discussion of this problem see Stanley E. Boyle, "The Average Concentration Ratio: An Inappropriate Measure of Structure," *The Journal of Political Economy,* 1971; and D. Bailey, S. E. Boyle, C. McKnew and R. C. Sorensen, "Statistical Problems Encountered in the Development of Weighted Three-Digit Concentration Ratios from Bureau of the Census Four-Digit Industry Data," *1969 Proceedings of the Business and Economic Statistics Section of the American Statistical Association,* December 1969, pp. 685–688.

[25] *Ibid.,* p. 687.

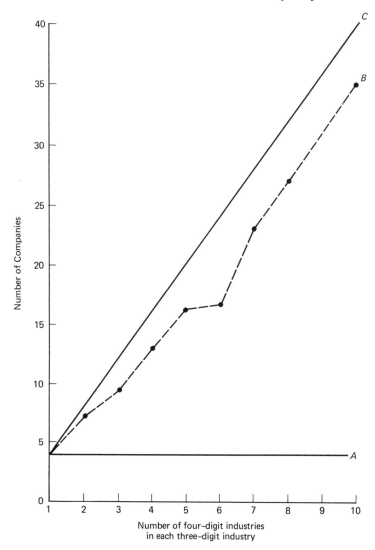

A — Minimum possible number of firms
B — Actual number of firms. There were no three-digit industries for which data
were available which had exactly nine four-digit industries in them
C — Maximum possible number of firms

Figure 5-4   The Distribution of the Leading Firms in 3-Digit and
4-Digit Industries: 1950

Concentration and Wage Levels

A second element of the performance of highly concentrated industries which has received some attention in the past few years has been
the relationship between the level of wages or unionization and the

level of concentration.[26] Since the arguments with respect to the effect of concentration and unionization upon wages are similar, attention will be directed to the relationship between wage levels and degree of monopoly (concentration).

As might be imagined, the positions adopted in this area represent the two polar extremes: High levels of concentration in industries result in low wage levels, or high wage levels. The proponents of the low wage thesis suggest that because of the financial strength of monopolies, wages in monopolized (high concentration) industries should be somewhat lower than those in competitive (low concentration) industries employing workers with essentially the same type or the same mix of skills. On the other hand, other studies have appeared which suggest a positive relationship between the degree of monopoly power and the level of wages. The latter studies assume that firms with substantial monopoly power do, because of their high profit position, give their workers higher wages than they might obtain in industries earning more competitive levels of profits. This argument suggests that the absence of competitive pressures enables and perhaps encourages firms to be somewhat lax in their attempts to keep costs at a low level. Thus it is suggested that rather than wage rates being lower in monopolized industries, they are higher. This assumes that monopolists prefer to pay high wages, or perhaps they feel better able to absorb higher wages and pass them on consumers.

In 1960, Schwartzman presented an interesting test of the wage level-concentration relationship.[27] Because of the differential effects that such variables as skill levels, labor supply and unionization, as well as the level of concentration may have on inter-industry wage level comparisons, he compared sets of identical industries in two countries—Canada and the United States. The purpose of this process was to isolate the effect of monopoly power upon wages.

> Since technology in the two countries is similar, the skills employed by any industry will be the same. . . . Technological similarity and similarities in industrial patterns of training ensure that supply elasticities will not differ greatly between companies.[28]

In addition Schwartzman attempted to adjust for differences in national labor policy. The analysis includes three sets of wage level comparisons:

---

[26] See J. W. Garbarino, "A Theory of Inter-Industry Wage Variation," *Quarterly Journal of Economics*, May 1950, pp. 299–305; G. J. Stigler, "The Statistics of Monopoly and Merger," *Journal of Political Economy*, February 1956, pp. 33–40; D. Schwartzman, "Monopoly and Wages," *The Canadian Journal of Economics and Political Science*, August 1960, pp. 428–438; and L. Weiss, "Concentration and Labor Earnings," *American Economic Review*, March 1966, pp. 96–117.

[27] Schwartzman, "Monopoly and Wages," *op. cit.*

[28] *Ibid.*, p. 436.

(1) between industries of low concentration in both countries, (2) between industries of high concentration in both countries, and (3) between industries which show high levels of concentration in Canada but low levels in the United States.[29]

Primary interest is in the last group *if* a wage effect of monopoly power is to be seen. Using the first group to standardize for differences in national wage policy, the ratio of average wages for the third group in the two countries (Canada/United States) was .77. The relative wage ratio for the industries included in the second group was .81 and was not statistically significant from the first group's. Thus, Schwartzman concluded that there was no measurable or significant effect of differences in monopoly power upon wages.

Care should be exercised in the uncritical acceptance of the results of the Schwartzman analysis. One major problem is that the sample included only 17 industries; more important, however, is the fact that the industries included were rather insignificant. Clearly the results shed little light on the basic question: Does monopoly raise wages?

In 1966, Weiss approached the problem from a somewhat different point of view. He pointed out, for example, that even in competitive markets some employers may pay more for workers than others and in return they may obtain "correspondingly superior workers." [30] However, many doubt that all or the major part of inter-industry wage differentials can be explained fully by differences in employee productivity. In an attempt to shed new light in this area, he attempts to test two major hypotheses. First, "that concentrated industries pay higher annual rates of labor for particular 'occupations'." Second, "that these high earnings are more than can be accounted for by the personal characteristics of the labor employed." [31] Unlike Schwartzman who used the *Census of Manufactures*, Weiss used the *1960 Census of Population* for his basic wage data.

The basic model used by Weiss included three variables: Y is annual earnings, CR is the concentration ratio, and U is the extent of collective bargaining coverage.

$$Y = b_0 + b_1 CR + b_2 U + b_3 U \cdot CR \tag{5-1}$$

Thus, the existence of monopoly wages is assumed to be a function of "concentrated and/or unionized industries." [32] Positive coefficients for b_1

---

[29] The dividing line falls roughly at a 4-firm concentration ratio of 50 percent.

[30] L. Weiss, "Concentration and Labor Earnings," *op. cit.*, p. 97.

[31] *Ibid.*, pp. 97–98.

[32] Other variables are also considered subsequently. These include industries in which employment is increasing rapidly, the difference between durable and nondurable goods, the size of the employer, and the overall labor force characteristics (sex, skill level, race, geographic location, and urban-rural characteristics). These will not be treated separately here.

and b_2 and a negative coefficient for b_3 support the argument. On the other hand, if b_1 and b_3 are both negative the hypotheses would have to be rejected. Thus, the signs of the three coefficients can be taken as a guide to the accuracy of the hypotheses.

A brief explanation of the simple (two variable) least-squares regression was presented earlier in this chapter. The analysis here introduces other variables into the problem. It is referred to, therefore, as multiple regression analysis. It recognizes that variables other than level of concentration may affect wage levels. This approach makes it possible to appraise the contribution of each variable and the sum of all the variables to an explanation of differential wage levels.

Looking first at the results obtained while examining male production workers, Weiss concluded that "Unionization seems to raise annual earnings by about 16 percent when concentration is low, but to have no effect when (concentration) is high." He also found that "Concentration seems to raise earnings by about 33 percent when unions are weak, but by only 13 percent when they are strong." Thus, "monopoly rents could be very large." [33] As other variables depicting labor force characteristics are added, the effect of both concentration and the degree of unionization appear to decline. Using his basic model Weiss concluded that $r^2 = .04$. Reference to this earlier discussion of correlation analysis indicates that the result is statistically significant but that the variables included do not explain much of the variation in wage rates.

In all, Weiss tested the effect of some 30 to 40 different labor force characteristic variables upon differential wage rates. In the end he concluded that his *first* hypothesis seems to be the best, and that the relationship was the strongest in the case of male production workers. He found little support for his second hypothesis. His conclusion is most significant.

> All of the conclusions of this paper are necessarily tentative because the indexes of concentration used are imperfect, because industry definitions are arbitrary, because weights used in combining markets to match Census industries are arbitrary, and because the Census places some persons in the wrong industries.[34]

The possible errors associated with the first problem (the quality of the concentration index) are so large as to erase any positive correlation which may have been found. We have already shown that average indexes such as those used by Weiss, Miller, Kilpatrick and others cannot give accurate estimates of the degree of concentration in the larger three-digit industries. Given the magnitude of the error resulting from these computations of the weighted concentration index, and the small

[33] *Ibid.*, pp. 104–105.
[34] *Ibid.*, p. 116.

value for r^2, it is quite reasonable to conclude that there is no proven relationship between the variables.

In an effort to overcome some of the shortcomings of the two studies which have been examined, an attempt has been made by the author to deal more directly with the basic question: Are wages in highly concentrated industries higher than those in industries where concentration is low? This analysis uses *1963 Census of Manufactures* data for 417 industry classifications.[35] The analysis assumes that (1) a positive and significant relationship exists between wages and level of concentration, and (2) that a similar and perhaps equivalent relationship exists between wage levels and productivity.

The three-variable multiple regression model assumes that annual wages are function of degree of monopoly and labor productivity.

$$Y = a + bCR_4 + cP \tag{5-2}$$

Y is annual wages per production worker, CR_4 is the simple 4-firm concentration ratio,[36] and P is a proxy for productivity (shipments per man hour). The shortcomings of shipments per man hour as a proxy for productivity are obvious. On the other hand, the difficulty of rearranging the data published by the Bureau of the Census, with the attendant errors, suggests that it may be a usable first approximation. The signs of b and c should be positive.

The results of this examination were quite interesting. The following results were obtained using all 417 4-digit industry groups without adjustment for "market-basket" categories and other similar problems. Looking first at the simple relationship between the level of wages and concentration:

$$Y = 4150.5 + .0189CR, \text{ where } r^2 = .35 \tag{5-3}$$

Between wage level and productivity a similar relationship is seen.

$$Y = 4388.1 + .0270P \text{ where } r^2 = .34 \tag{5-4}$$

Combining the three variables:

$$Y = 3897.2 + .0153CR + .0215P, \text{ where } r = .651 \ r^2 = .439 \tag{5-5}$$

[35] It unfortunately does not allow for an examination of wage differentials for similar types of occupations in different industries. The results have not been put into any formal form.

[36] A variety of other indexes were constructed and used in the analysis, including a variety of cumulative indexes, eight-firm concentration ratios and the like. In no case was there a significant difference in the results.

While this is admittedly a simple test, it has the advantage that it does not require any massive recalculation of the data. Moreover, it appears to yield larger and more significant r^2 values than the other studies which have been examined. The results obtained substantiate both of the hypotheses suggested. First, there is a statistically significant relationship between levels of wages and concentration. It is positive and it is clear. Second, it appears that the productivity plays an almost equally important role exerting a significant and positive influence upon wage levels. These results show in a less ambiguous manner than do the other studies that concentration does exert a significant influence upon the level of wages.

Concentration and Advertising

In recent years the relationship between product differentiation (advertising) expenditures and concentration has obtained considerable attention. Many have alleged that large and prolonged advertising expenditures are positively correlated with monopoly power. The arguments suggest a possible effect on both the supply and demand sides of the market. The major argument on the supply side of the market revolves around the presence or absence of substantial economies of scale in advertising.[37] To a lesser degree, suggestions have been made that large advertising expenditures may make success in a market dependent upon the firm's ability to meet high absolute cost requirements. If either effect is present, then existing large firms have decided advantages over small firms or new firms, in that large advertisers are able to obtain greater advertising impact per dollars of expenditure than small ones.[38] On the demand side, prolonged advertising may have the effect of developing strong brand loyalties. This would result in making the demand for the product of the large advertiser more inelastic (less responsive to price changes), and raise the barriers to entry facing new firms.

In a review of the empirical results obtained with respect to the presence of scale effects in advertising, Preston concluded that: (1) There are reasons to expect that scale economics in advertising may exist; (2) There are many examples which show falling advertising and sales ratios with increasing firm size; and (3) "There is no general and perva-

---

[37] The results obtained from these studies appear to be inconclusive. L. Telser, "Advertising and Competition," *The Journal of Political Economy*, December 1964, pp. 537–562; J. L. Simon, "Are There Economies of Scale in Advertising?", *Journal of Advertising Research*, June 1965, pp. 15–20; D. Blank, "Television Advertising: The Great Discount Illusion, or Tonypanda Revisited," *Journal of Business*, January 1968, pp. 10–38; and J. L. Peterman, "The Clorox Case and Television Rate Structures," *The Journal of Law and Economics*, October 1968, pp. 321–422.

[38] L. E. Preston, "Advertising Effects and Public Policy," paper prepared for meetings of the American Marketing Association, August 1968, p. 3.

sive tendency for large-scale advertising activity to be accompanied by the achievement of substantial economics of scale. . . ." [39]

On the other hand, recent studies of the relationship between changes in concentration and advertising show somewhat more positive results. We have already looked at one study which examines both the direction and magnitude of changes in concentration in producer good and consumer good industries between 1947 and 1966.[40] In the consumer good area, industries were subdivided on the basis of the extent of product differentiation present in each. It showed, for example, that concentration increased less in producer good than in consumer good industries, and that it increased more in highly differentiated consumer good industries than in any other area (Table 5-2). The results of this study were clear. There is a strong and positive relationship between the two variables.

Table 5-2   Changes in Concentration
in 213 Manufacturing Industries: 1947–1966

Type of Industry	Number of Industries[a]	Concentration		
		Increased	Same[b]	Decreased
		Percent		
Producer goods	132	31	24	45
Consumer goods	81	58	20	22
Highly differentiated	17	82	—	18
Moderately differentiated	36	58	25	17
Undifferentiated	28	43	25	32

[a] 213 industries for which comparable industry classifications exist over this period.

[b] Change of plus or minus 3 percentage points.

Source: *Studies by the Staff of the Cabinet Committee on Price Stability*, January 1969, p. 59.

Another interesting approach to the problem has been taken in a series of studies by Michael Mann.[41] Using individual company data, he attempts to measure empirically the relationship between advertising and concentration. A problem of such studies is the development of a

[39] *Ibid*, pp. 14–15.

[40] W. F. Mueller, "Statement," *Hearings before the Senate Select Committee on Small Business*, March 15, 1967, p. 69.

[41] M. Mann, "Seller Concentration, Barriers to Entry, and Rates of Return in 30 Industries, 1950–1960," *The Review of Economics and Statistics*, August 1966, pp. 296–307; M. Mann, "Asymmetry, Barriers to Entry and Rates of Return in Twenty-Six Concentrated Industries, 1948 to 1957," *Western Economic Journal*, March 1970, pp. 86–89; and Mann, Henning and Meehan, 'Advertising and Concentration: An Empirical Investigation," *Journal of Industrial Economics*, November 1967, pp. 34–45.

measure of advertising intensity. Most studies use a ratio of advertising expenditures to sales or shipments. Under normal circumstances these estimates may be quite acceptable but they may contain some problems. First, many firms employ promotional methods which are not accurately classified as advertising costs. Second, data that are available from such places as *Advertising Age* include expenditures for advertising in only a limited list of outlets. Most notably they ignore local advertising. Finally, most firms which are large enough to be included in any discussion of the impact of advertising expenditures upon the level of concentration are usually large and diversified companies. As such, their advertising expenditures data are compared with their sales for the full range of the products they sell. Thus, they tend to understate advertising concentration in particular product markets.

Mann attempted to overcome these problems by using national firms which were engaged primarily (more than half of their total revenue) in the manufacture of a single product line, like tires, beer, bread, and cereal. Despite the fact that each company is a leader in its field, some manufacture other products. Tire producers, for example, produce synthetic rubber and industrial rubber products. Despite these problems, Mann was able to test the relationship between advertising expenditures and concentration in 14 industries for 1954, 1958 and 1963. The results suggest that the correlation between concentration and advertising is positive and statistically significant.[42]

The conclusions of these and other studies of advertising and concentration might be summarized by the following statement.

> Advertising expenditures of high product differentiation industries have increased at a faster rate than those of either the moderate or low product differentiation industries. Moreover, large companies increase their advertising expenditures at a faster rate than the small companies . . .[43]

Excess Capacity

A useful but seldom used measure of "real" industry performance is the presence of long-run excess capacity in an industry. The significance to be attached to this variable is conditioned by three factors: What type of excess capacity is present in the industry? What has been the rate of growth of output of the industry? What has happened with respect to entry into the industry?

Excess capacity may be of two types, "peak load," and "on stream" capacity. In the first instance, an unused plant may exist which is used simply to meet "peak load" demands for the product. In such cases, the

[42] *Ibid.*, pp. 37–38.
[43] FTC, *The Structure of Food Manufacturing, op. cit.*, p. 200.

machinery may be old and inefficient, and differ considerably from the regular plant and equipment used by the firm. The other case, however, is one where usual production capacity exceeds demand by a considerable amount in the long run. If the second type of long-run excess capacity exists, it may represent a malfunction of the market.

The competitive significance to be attributed to the presence of excess capacity depends, in part, upon the rate of growth in output for the industry. If output remains almost constant or declines over some long period, one might expect capacity to exceed demand throughout this period. If, on the other hand, production has grown steadily and substantially, the presence of long-run excess capacity might be inferred to be a part of the response of present industry members to the threat of potential entry.

The interpretation to be placed upon the importance of industry growth is conditioned by the entrance of new firms into the industry. If the number of firms in the industry remains unchanged for long periods, despite the growth of production and the presence of substantial excess capacity, one might suspect that industry performance deviated from that which might be hoped for from a more competitive market. Firms in such situations may be guilty of what has been referred to as the preemptive building of capacity, that is, building capacity in advance so as to keep new firms out of the industry. To test the validity of this assumption one would want to examine the relationship between actual and optimum size firms. If they correspond closely the allegation would appear to be without merit. If data were available on an individual firm basis one would clearly want to examine the relative incidence of excess capacity to determine the extent to which it was an individualized or industry-wide phenomenon.

The presence of substantial long-run excess capacity is not often included in an analysis of the performance of industry. The reason for this is simple. It requires that data be available which show firm and industry production and capacity. Figures for capacity are seldom available. The major exception to this is in a limited number of industries which produce products which are largely undifferentiated. A careful reading of the synthetic rubber case study in the next chapter suggests that when data are available to measure the presence of excess capacity, it can be a useful addition to the analytical tools with which to appraise the performance of an industry.

SUMMARY

As we have seen, there are formidable problems which are encountered when one attempts to measure the performance of an industry. In part this stems from the fact that economists have been rather casual about the construction and use of variables to depict industry structure and performance. To some extent these errors of basic logic have compounded the problems of tracing out cause-effect relationships.

Despite the shortcomings of the available data it has been possible to illustrate some of the relationships which exist between such performance variables as rates of profits, wage levels, advertising expenditures and industry structure. In most cases, the relationships examined do not appear to be strong; structure as measured by concentration does not explain much of the variation in performance. Moreover, the measures which are used are far from perfect. The fact remains, however, that the studies referred to do provide some empirical verification of relationships between structure and performance of the type predicted by economic theory.

The data show that profit levels are higher in industries when the level of concentration is high than it is in those where the level of concentration is low. Although most studies are of the cross-section type, this is apparently true in both the short run and the long run. The more accurate the measure of concentration, the clearer the relationship appears to be. The clearest case in point is the FTC *Report on Food Manufacturing,* which obtained high r^2 values using excellent data.

Wage levels appear to be positively related to the level of concentration. Average annual wages increase as the level of concentration increases. It is true, however, that wages are also correlated positively with productivity. Viewing both sets of studies, it is clear that monopoly power does have the effect of permitting permanent distortions of ideal cost-price relationships. Misallocation of resources exists and unless these general conclusions are substantially in error, it is present to a significant degree.

Finally it is clear that large advertising and related expenditures are positively correlated with high levels of concentration and that they probably serve to perpetuate or enhance the misallocation which currently exists in industries characterized by high levels of product differentiation. As Bain pointed out, strong product differentiation does act as an effective barrier to entry and results in the perpetuation of monopoly power.

The material reviewed in this and the three preceding chapters is used to analyze these industries in Chapter 6. This chapter has demonstrated a type of approach that can be made to the analysis of the state of competition in individual industries, as well as the type of data which are necessary. A final hope is that it will suggest ways in which the researcher may adopt existing data for such purposes.

6

CASE STUDIES IN COMPETITION

Industrial organization can be approached from many angles. Some students are interested in the trend of specified activities (merger activity, for example) through time, while others find variations in the use of a particular device in different industrial areas of more interest. The most interesting aspect to others, particularly to those who might best be described as antitrust practitioners, is the application of analytical tools to the study of particular situations. These studies are often the most interesting as they include the entire spectrum of problems which occur in this area. Antitrust agencies are called upon on a day to day basis to reach conclusions regarding the competitive effects of particular joint promotional plans, various types of discount arrangements, advertising product claims, interlocking directorates, a merger or group of mergers, and a variety of other actions. In each case, this determination must be made within some product or industry frame of reference. Typically, a finding of injury includes a demonstration that an individual firm, or group of firms, has been damaged, moreover, that the alleged damage could be measured in some objective market.

Thus far, we have seen that it is possible to associate certain types of industry performance with underlying industry structure and conduct. The impact of a particular action will often vary depending upon individual market conditions. A merger's effects are not always the same.

Mergers among firms in industries which are atomistically structured often go unnoticed, and in fact have little effect upon the performance of the industry. In an industry where there are only a few sellers, the same action might well be considered to be damaging to competition. On the other hand, if the financial ability of smaller companies in a highly concentrated industry is weak, further concentration might be encouraged if merger activity were to establish the continuation of a viable firm rather than the disappearance of *all* of the smaller predecessor companies. This philosophy was certainly apparent in the approval by the antitrust agencies of the mergers which resulted in the formation of American Motors and in the acquisition of Packard by Studebaker. The first appears to have had some success while the latter was a failure; it is apparent that antitrust policy cannot be a substitute for good business practices and sound financial backing. Experience shows, however, that only a minor portion of all mergers fit in this category.

In each case where it is necessary to make conclusions regarding the competitive effect of a particular action or a series of related actions, it is both desirable and necessary to have an accurate picture of the economic setting within which it is taking place. It is necessary to know the major structural characteristics of the industry, the form which inter-firm competition has taken in the past, and the resulting performance of the industry. If knowledge of these factors is available, it is possible to provide a more informed estimate of the consequences of any proposed course of action.

In actual market situations, unless the researcher has unusual data collection powers,[1] these decisions must be made on the basis of incomplete information. This should not prove to be too frightening a prospect, since all decisions of any importance should be made on this basis. The important thing, however, is that a minimum of information must be available which will show at least the major characteristics of the market in question. These need not be the same factors in each market, although many of them will be the same.[2] The following case studies are designed to assist the student in identifying and appraising the types of interrelationships which have been discussed in the preceding chapters.

[1] Aside from the Bureau of the Census, the most extensive data collection powers in government are possessed by the antitrust agencies—Antitrust Division, Department of Justice and the Federal Trade Commission. Section 6 of the Federal Trade Commission Act reads in part, "That the commission should also have power—(a) To gather and compile information concerning, and to investigate from time to time the organization, business, conduct, practices, and management of any corporation engaged in commerce and its relation to other corporations and to individuals, associations, and partnerships."

[2] For one of the most extensive lists of possible areas of examination see Stephen H. Sosnick, "A Critique of Concepts of Workable Competition," *The Quarterly Journal of Economics*, August 1958, pp. 380–423. This treatment illustrates the problems encountered in undertaking a detailed examination of all of the trees in the forest in the absence of any idea of the dimensions of the basic problem.

[3] The bulk of the material contained in this section is taken from two articles by the author: "Government Promotion of Monopoly Power: An Examination of the Sale of the Synthetic Rubber Industry," *The Journal of Industrial Economics*, April

THE SYNTHETIC RUBBER INDUSTRY [3]

Prior to the start of World War II, natural rubber was used almost exclusively in this country. Total synthetic rubber production totaled only 8,000 tons in 1941. With the invasion and occupation of all of Southeast Asia by the Japanese in 1941 and 1942, almost all natural rubber production came under their control. Some basic technique was available for the production of synthetic rubber from petroleum byproducts and industrial alcohol. Under the direction of the Federal government, and with a large-scale investment program, a massive synthetic rubber production program was undertaken. By 1945, new (synthetic) rubber production in the United States totaled over 830,000 long tons. This would have to be considered a successful program by almost any standard.

During World War II and for the next ten years the bulk of all synthetic rubber production was in the hands of the Federal government, but operated on contract by private companies. All major price and investment decisions were made by the government. Immediately following the war, plans were drafted for the transfer of the industry to private hands. At first, private firms showed little interest in the operation of the industry, but with an improved product and rapidly rising natural rubber prices during the Korean War, considerable pressure was generated in an effort to hasten the sale of the production facilities to private industry. This finally occurred in May of 1955. Total synthetic rubber production was about 982,000 long tons in 1955. Our interest here is in the period from 1955 to 1964, the first ten years of private operation.

Industry Growth

Between 1955 and 1964, United States synthetic rubber production increased from 982,000 long tons to almost 1.8 million long tons or by about 80 percent (Table 6–1), and the value of shipments of all synthetic rubber increased by more than 125 percent.[4] In 1964, the total value of synthetic rubber shipments was almost $820 million. Over the same period, the production of S-type rubber alone increased from about 800,000 long tons to over 1.25 million long tons.[5]

1961, pp. 151–169; and "The Synthetic Rubber Industry: 1955–64, A Case Study of Limited Competition," *The Antitrust Bulletin*, Spring 1968, pp. 83–103.

[4] U.S. Bureau of the Census, *Census of Manufactures*, 1963, *Industry Statistics: Plastics Materials, Synthetic Rubber, and Man-Made Fibers*, MC 63 (2)-28B Table 1; *Annual Survey of Manufactures* 1965, *General Statistics for Industry Groups and Industries*, M65 (AS)-1, Table 1.

[5] In 1964, total synthetic rubber production was divided as follows: S-type rubber (74 percent), butyl rubber (5 percent), neoprene rubber (7.5 percent), N-type rubber (3 percent) and other rubbers (10 percent). *Second Report of the Attorney General on Competition in the Synthetic Rubber*, p. 6; and *Tenth Report of the Attorney General on Competition in the Synthetic Rubber Industry*, p. 9. Hereafter referred to as *First Report, Second Report*, and so on.

Table 6-1   Synthetic Rubber Production: 1955 and 1960–1964
(thousands of long tons)

Year	S-Type	Butyl	Neoprene	N-Type	Other[a]	Total[b]
1955	801	56	91	33	—	982
1960	1166	98	134	38	—	1,436
1961	1110	88	119	41	47	1,404
1962	1194	90	129	46	116	1,574
1963	1159	108	129	48	164	1,608
1964	1255	99	141	52	217	1,765

[a] Primarily polybutadiene and polyisoprene.
[b] Detail may not equal totals because of rounding.
Source: Compiled from U.S. Department of Commerce, *Rubber: Supply and Distribution for the U.S., Summary for 1964*, Current Industrial Reports, Series M30A (64)-13, Table 1; and U.S. Department of Commerce, *United States Rubber Statistics*, April 10, 1958, pp. 2–5.

Total synthetic rubber production has increased by slightly more than 10 percent a year since 1955; moreover, its share of total rubber consumption has increased. In 1955, synthetic rubber accounted for 59 percent of total United States rubber consumption, but by 1964, it had increased to about 75 percent.

Two factors are responsible for this basic shift: (1) the increased acceptability of synthetic rubber by rubber products manufacturers; and (2) the development of the stereo rubbers polybutadiene and polyisoprene whose chemical and physical characteristics parallel those of natural rubber.

The development of the stereo rubbers resulted in a modest decline in the relative importance of the older types of synthetic rubber. Between 1956 and 1964, for example, S-type rubber declined from 81 percent to 74 percent of total synthetic rubber production, butyl declined from 7 percent to 5 percent, and neoprene's share declined from 9 percent to 7.5 percent. Despite the modest decline in S-type rubber production, it remains seven times that of the next largest type and accounts for almost three-fourths of total synthetic rubber production.[6]

Thus, while S-type rubber production increased by 57 percent between 1955 and 1964, productive capacity increased by 89 percent. The bulk of this increase occurred prior to 1960, remaining rather stable after 1960. During the same period, capacity increased by about 15 percent, or by more than 200,000 long tons.

[6] By 1969 S-type rubber accounted for 66.5 percent of total synthetic production, while the share of the stereo rubbers had increased to 19.4 percent. Despite its declining share of the total, S-type rubber consumption increased by about 45 percent between 1960 and 1969. U.S. Department of Commerce, Business and Defense Services Administration, *U.S. Industrial Outlook: 1970*, December 1969, pp. 195–196.

New Entrants

The conditions of entry are particularly important in an industry composed of only a few firms. Despite the fact that S-type rubber production and capacity increased at a rapid rate between 1955 and 1964 (45 percent and 89 percent respectively), the industry has experienced little in the way of new entry. Between 1955 and 1964, for example, only three firms entered into the production of S-type rubber.[7] Moreover, these new entrants accounted for less than 8 percent of 1964 S-type production.

An examination of the industry suggests that barriers to entry of the usual types are not present in the production of S-type rubber. Economies of scale are not large. However, existing plants vary in size from 2 percent to 9 percent of industry capacity and are somewhat larger than the average of all manufacturing plants. In 1964, plants of new entrants accounted for only 3 percent of total industry capacity. In addition, there do not appear to be any significant multiplant economies of scale. Access to the major raw materials is easy, and patents and technical knowledge are generally available and do not provide a major obstacle to entry. There is a barrier to entry, however; it is access to customers. Available data indicate that this is a substantial barrier.

Table 6-2   Distribution of Domestic S-Type Sales,
by Type of Customer: 1957–1964
(as a percent of total domestic sales)

Year	Intra-Company Transfers	Sales to Affiliates or Constituent Companies	"Big Five"[a]	All Other	Total
1957	29.9	23.4	12.4	34.3	100.0
1960	27.8	27.3	7.4	37.5	100.0
1962	30.1	27.2	5.8	36.9	100.0
1964	32.7	29.1	6.2	32.0	100.0

[a] General Tire Company, Goodrich Rubber Company, Goodyear Tire and Rubber Co., Firestone Tire and Rubber Company, and United States Rubber Company.
Source: *Third Report*, p. 19; *Sixth Report*, p. 15; *Eighth Report*, p. 13; and *Tenth Report*, p. 22.

One measure of the importance of this limitation can be obtained by examining recent changes in the size of the "open" market for S-type rubber. The data in Table 6-2 show the distribution of domestic S-type

[7] Two of the firms (W. R. Grace & Co., Dewey & Almy Chem. Div. and General Tire & Rubber) were new to the industry; the third (International Latex) was a producer of N-type Rubber. In 1964 there were two butyl rubber producers compared with one in 1955. The new producer was Columbian Carbon Division of Cities Services Co., Inc.

rubber sales by class of customer for selected years. They show that both intra-company transfers and sales to affiliates and subsidiaries have increased rather sharply since 1960. In 1957, these two customer classes accounted for 53.3 percent of domestic sales. By 1964, they accounted for 61.8 percent of domestic sales, an increase of 8.5 percent.

Most notable from a competitive point of view is the decline of open market S-type rubber sales, particularly since 1960 (from 37.5 percent to 32.0 percent). This decline represents both a relative and actual decline in the size of the market. The shrinking size of the open market suggests that new entry into the industry is likely to be difficult.

Table 6-3   Distribution of Estimates of Industry Capacity: 1964

COMPANY	PERCENT	CUMULATIVE PERCENT
Goodyear	18.2	18.2
Goodrich-Gulf[a]	16.5	34.7
Firestone Tire and Rubber	16.4	51.1
Texas-U.S. Rubber[b]	9.4	60.5
Copolymer[c]	8.0	68.5
Phillips Petroleum	6.6	75.1
Shell Oil Company	6.3	81.4
American Synthetic Rubber Corp.[d]	6.0	87.4
United Carbon[e]	4.7	92.1
General Tire	4.3	96.4
U.S. Rubber	1.9	98.3
Other[f]	1.6	99.9

[a] Joint venture of B. F. Goodrich and Gulf Oil Company.
[b] Joint venture of Texaco and U.S. Rubber Company.
[c] Joint venture of the Armstrong Rubber Company, the Gates Rubber Company, the Mansfield Tire and Rubber Company, and the Sieberling Rubber Company.
[d] Joint venture of 26 rubber products manufacturers.
[e] Subsidiary of Ashland Oil and Refining.
[f] Includes Dewey and Alma Chemical Company (Division of W. R. Grace and Company) and International Latex Corporation.
SOURCE: *Tenth Report.*

Changes in Concentration

One of the more crucial structural variables affecting an industry's competitive performance is the degree of concentration. Bain points out that:

"High" or "very high" seller concentration in an industry generally seems to be conducive to poor performance in the crucial matter of price-cost relations or profits, without evidently bestowing offsetting advantages in other dimensions of market performance.[8]

[8] Joe S. Bain, *op. cit.*, p. 423, note 5.

A brief examination of recent concentration level changes in highly concentrated, producer good industries may assist in appraising similar changes in the synthetic rubber industry. The production of S-type rubber is highly concentrated; it has also been quite stable. Moreover, the industry is populated by firms ranked among the largest in the country. Seven firms in the industry have assets of $1 billion or more; three have assets of $500 million to $999 million; and two have assets of $100 million to $99 million: *Moody's Industrial Manual*, 1965. An additional five firms are closely held joint ventures of very large chemical and petroleum producers for which accurate asset values are not published. The major producers of S-type rubber are arrayed as shown in Table 6-3.

The data in Table 6-4 show that: (1) irrespective of the variable selected, the share of the five leading firms was relatively stable between 1955 and 1964; and (2) the share controlled by the five leading companies showed little variation on an annual basis among the three variables.

Table 6-4   Share of Domestic Sales, Capacity and Production of S-Type Rubber Controlled by the Five Leading Companies: 1955–1964 (as percent of industry total)

VARIABLE	1955	1956	1957	1958	1959	1960	1961	1962	1963	1964
Dom. Sales	74	74	72	70	69	71	70	69	70	71
Capacity [a]	70	76	70	71	70	70	69	69	68	69
Production	72	74	75	73	71	72	73	71	[b]	[b]

[a] Year-end capacity.
[b] Production concentration data for 1963 and 1964 were collected but were not published by the Department of Justice.
Source: *Report of the Attorney General on Competition in the Synthetic Rubber Industry*, various issues, 1956 through 1965.

Excess Capacity

While S-type rubber production increased by 57 percent between 1955 and 1964, productive capacity increased at an even faster rate. The net result of these changes is that the level of excess S-type capacity in 1964 exceeded that of 1955 (Table 6-5), and was high throughout the period. Substantial unused capacity may exist for a variety of reasons; however, if it persists over the long run, particularly while output increases, it suggests that competition is not particularly active.

Bain has pointed out, for example, that "considerable chronic excess capacity not justified by secular change or reasonable standby provision" was a sign of unworkable competition.[9] An examination of annual

[9] Joe S. Bain, "Workable Competition in Oligopoly: Theoretical Considerations and Some Empirical Evidence," *The American Economic Review*, May 1950, p. 37.

rates of S-type capacity utilization indicates that considerable excess capacity existed between 1956 and 1964. The data presented in Table 6-5 show that capacity utilization reached as high as 65 percent in only four of the ten years. Thus, by 1964 the condition might well be referred to as chronic.

Table 6-5   Unused S-Type Rubber Producing Capacity: 1955–1964 (capacity minus production as a percent of capacity)

Year	Percent [a]	Year	Percent [a]
1955	17.3	1960	34.1
1956	26.9	1961	41.4
1957	40.4	1962	37.3
1958	44.5	1963	41.0
1959	33.5	1964	38.3

[a] The use of year-end rather than average capacity figures introduces a slight upward bias in the figures. In recent years, annual additions to capacity have been smaller, thereby diminishing the problem.
Source: *Report of the Attorney General on Competition in the Synthetic Rubber Industry*, various issues.

Price Movements

Given the fact that S-type rubber is an undifferentiated product, it is not surprising that at any given point in time all producers will sell it at the same price. This is to be expected. The unique feature of S-type rubber prices is their almost complete invariability through time. In the words of the Attorney General:

> The most significant unfavorable competition factor over the past ten years has been the virtually complete absence of open price responsiveness to changing market conditions. . . . the general price structure has remained uniform and unchanged for over almost the whole period; these ignore rubber prices and the softness of a buyer's market.[10]

To this it should be added that stable prices were maintained in the face of increasing excess capacity.

Profits

Economic theory tells us that, other things being equal, profits and profit margins will be larger under monopolistic conditions than under competitive conditions. We have examined a number of attempts to measure this relationship.

[10] *Tenth Report*, p. 36.

An approach developed by Schwartzman examines the difference between total revenue (value of shipments) and direct costs (payroll, cost of materials, cost of fuel consumed and purchased electricity) and it may be used as an index of industry profits.[11] This method does not attempt to measure the actual rate of profit. Instead it has been used as an indicator of changes in profit levels through time. The profit index is used in this industry because of the fact that actual profit data are not available for synthetic rubber producers. As the data in Table 6-3 indicate, there is no firm which is engaged primarily in this industry; the production of synthetic rubber is incidental to their other activities. As a consequence, a proxy for profit must be used.

The data presented in Table 6-6 indicate that between 1956 and 1965, the profit index for synthetic rubber increased by some 19 percentage points (about 14 percent), from 135 to 154.

Table 6-6 Distribution of Profit Indexes for Highly Concentrated Industries: 1956, 1960 and 1964 (as percent of industries reporting in each year)

PROFIT INDEX	1956	1960	1964
More than 3 percentage points above synthetic rubber *PI*	45.0	46.6	32.8
Plus or minus 3 percentage points of synthetic rubber *PI*	7.5	5.1	17.2
More than 3 percentage points below synthetic rubber *PI*	47.5	48.3	50.0

Source: Computed from U.S. Bureau of the Census, *Census of Manufactures,* 1963, *Industry Statistics, Plastics Materials, Synthetic Rubber and Man-Made Fibers* MC 63 (2)-28B, Table 1; and U.S. Bureau of the Census, *Annual Survey of Manufactures,* 1965, *General Statistics for Industry Groups and Industries,* M 65 (AS)-1, Table 1.

An appreciation of these data requires a comparison of the PI for the synthetic rubber industry with those of other industries also having high concentration ratios. In 1956, 45.0 percent of the highly concentrated industries were, by our measure, significantly more profitable than synthetic rubber; by 1964 only 32.8 percent of the concentrated industries surpassed the PI of synthetic rubber.[12]

[11] Schwartzman, *op. cit.,* p. 353. The profit index (*PI*) may be expressed as a relationship between value of shipments (*VS*) and direct costs (*DC*) or *PI-VS/DC.*

[12] The analysis includes the synthetic rubber industry (SIC 2822) and all other 4-digit industries in which the eight largest producers accounted for 80 percent or more of total industry value of shipments in 1963. Profit indexes were computed for the year 1956, 1960 and 1964.

Between 1956 and 1964, the synthetic rubber industry *PI* grew at a rate faster than that of other highly concentrated industries. Only nine of the industries included in the analysis showed a higher profit index growth rate than did the synthetic rubber industry.

The picture obtained of the synthetic rubber industry in this relatively brief examination is one of an industry which has experienced rapid increases in production and capacity. Despite the fact that value of shipment almost tripled between 1954 and 1966, concentration continues at a high level with the four largest S-type rubber producers accounting for 70 percent of total sales.

High and relatively stable levels of concentration are not the only indications of limited competition. Net entry into the industry has been slight and new entrants have accounted for a small share (5 percent) of industry sales. Two factors may be a part of this. First, excess capacity in the industry averaged about 35 percent in recent years. Existing firms have added capacity far in advance of the need for it. This may have the effect of discouraging new entrants not already engaged in rubber fabrication. Second, prices of S-type rubber were constant for the first 10 years of private operation. Such behavior has been described as administered pricing. It assumes some form of tacit or overt collusion among existing firms in the industry.

While actual profit data are not available for synthetic rubber producers, an examination of the industry profit index shows it to be high and rising in recent years. The results obtained come close to a classic description of the structure, conduct and performance of industries showing evidence of considerable monopoly power.

THE BAKING INDUSTRY

Despite the fact that more than 4,000 firms are engaged in the bread baking industry (SIC 2051), it has been the subject of a great amount of study, investigation and litigation charging anticompetitive behavior over the past 20 years.[13] A brief examination of an industry populated

[13] *Report of the Federal Trade Commission on Wholesale Baking Industry,* Parts I and II, 1946; R. G. Walsh and B. M. Evans, *Economics of Change in Market Structure, Conduct and Performance: The Baking Industry 1948–1958,* University of Nebraska Studies No. 28, 1963; National Commission on Food Marketing, *Organization and Competition in the Milling and Baking Industries,* Technical Study No. 5, 1966; Hearings before the Senate Subcommittee on Antitrust and Monopoly of the Committee on the Judiciary, *Administered Prices, Part 12, Study of Administered Prices in the Bread Industry,* 1959; and Federal Trade Commission, *Economic Report on the Baking Industry,* 1968. In addition to these recent studies, copies of a large number of decisions are available for cases in which baking companies have been the prosecuted for a number of actions involving alleged violations of the antimerger, price discrimination and price fixing statutes. Firms in the baking industry were defendants in almost 15 percent of all price fixing suits filed by the Department of Justice between 1950 and 1965 which involved food processing companies.

by such a large number of firms provides a vehicle markedly different from the synthetic rubber industry for the application of the basic techniques of industrial organization analysis. It shows, moreover, that there are some differences in the types of behavioral problems which develop in industries with many firms as compared with those which have only a small number of firms.

The Structure of the Industry

The bread and related products industry had shipments of about $4.7 billion in 1965.[14] It ranks, therefore, as one of the largest dozen industries in the country. By way of comparison, this was equal to about 70 percent of the value of all canned and frozen foods produced in 1965. These products account for an estimated 10 percent of all consumer food purchases. According to a study prepared for the National Commision on Food Marketing, shipments of bread and rolls account for 65 percent of the total value of shipments of the industry.[15] The remainder is distributed among sweet rolls, cake, pies and other pastry products.

According to the Bureau of the Census, shipments of bread and related products are produced primarily by wholesale bakers (78 percent) and grocery chains (11 percent).[16] The Census figures do not include products produced in single-unit retail bakeries or those produced by restaurants and other institutions primarily for consumption within the organization. These groups are not serious factors in the overall competition for bread sales.

Despite the size of the industry, it has experienced a relatively slow rate of growth in total shipments in recent years, and a decided reduction in *per capita* sales. For example, total white pan bread shipments increased by only 8 percent between 1947 and 1963, while *per capita* shipments actually declined from 64 pounds to 52 pounds per year or by about 19 percent.[17] Evans and Walsh point out that rising levels of consumer income and the development of new products have had the effect of substituting other carbohydrate products for bread in the diets of an increasing segment of the population.[18] Rising levels of retail bread prices (up 64 percent between 1950 and 1966) have contributed to the problem.[19]

Number and Size Distribution of Firms   In 1963, 4339 companies were engaged in the production of bread and related products. This

[14] Bureau of the Census, *Annual Survey of Manufactures, 1965.*
[15] NCFM, *Milling and Baking Industries, op. cit.,* p. 49.
[16] Bureau of the Census, *1963 Census of Manufactures.*
[17] FTC, *Economic Report on the Baking Industry, op. cit.,* p. 39.
[18] Evans and Walsh, *op. cit.,* p. 42.
[19] *Economic Report on Milk and Bread Prices, op. cit., passim.*

represented a 30 percent decline from the 5985 reported in 1947. Size of wholesale baking establishments and the changes in size which have occurred since 1947 are shown in Table 6-7.

Table 6-7   Distribution of Wholesale Baking Establishments
by Employment Size: 1947 and 1963

	Establishment				
	1947		*1963*		
Employment Size	Number	Percent	Number	Percent	Change
1–19	3,376	66	2,741	64	−625
20–99	1,323	26	990	23	−333
100–249	346	7	413	10	67
250 and over	74	1	143	3	69

Source: FTC, *Economic Report on the Baking Industry*, 1966, p. 40.

These data show that the brunt of the reduction in the number of baking companies was borne by the small, single-establishment baking company. Moreover, at the same time this decline occurred, there was an increase in the number of establishments with 100 or more employees (from 8 percent to 13 percent of all wholesale baking establishments).

Table 6-8   Average Number Baking Establishments
per Firm by Size Class: 1963

Size Class	Average Number Per Firm [a]
4 largest	58
Next 4 largest	29
Next 12 largest	8
Next 30 largest	4
Remaining 4289	1.04

[a] Figures rounded to nearest whole digit for first four categories.
Source: *Concentration Ratios in Manufacturing Industry: 1963*, Part II, Report of the Senate Subcommittee on Antitrust and Monopoly, 1967, Table 27, p. 360.

There is a clear relationship between the size of the firm and the number of baking establishments of that size operated (Table 6-8). The four largest baking companies operated a total of 232 baking establishments (an average of 58 per firm) and the 50 largest a total of 556 (an average of 11 per firm). The remaining 4289 firms operated a total of 4454 baking establishments or an average 1.04 establishment per firm. Since it is relatively rare for firms to operate more than one establishment in a given market area, it is obvious that the leading firms produce and sell in a wide variety of markets. Between 1952 and 1964 some 200 baking companies were acquired by other firms in the same industry. The bulk of the acquiring companies were large nation-wide producers.

The Level of Concentration Many questions were raised in Chapter 3 regarding the method employed in the collection of concentration data, as well as the appropriate geographic area to be used. These problems become clearer when the data available for the baking industry are examined.

Estimates provided by the Bureau of the Census indicate that concentration, while low, has increased steadily since 1947 (Table 6-9). The share of national industry shipments accounted for by the four largest companies increased from 16 percent in 1947 to 26 percent in 1967, an increase of ten percentage points or 62 percent. Almost all of the increase in concentration has been accounted for by the four largest firms. Firms ranked five through eight increased their share by two percentage points, while firms ranked nine through twenty showed no increase at all.

Table 6-9 Distribution of the Value of Bread and Related Product Shipment by Size Class of Firm: 1947, 1954, 1958, 1963, 1967

YEAR	FOUR LARGEST	NEXT FOUR LARGEST	EIGHT LARGEST	NEXT TWELVE LARGEST	TOTAL, TWENTY LARGEST
1947	16	10	26	10	36
1954	20	11	31	9	40
1958	22	11	33	9	42
1963	23	12	35	10	45
1967	26	12	38	9	47

Source: U.S. Bureau of the Census, *Census of Manufactures*, 1967, *Special Report, Concentration Ratios in Manufacturing*, Part I, MC 67(S)-2.1, p. SR 2–8.

Bread obviously is not shipped on a nationwide basis thus such concentration data considerably underestimate the *actual* levels of concentration in each geographic market. Despite these shortcomings, the existing census data estimates of industry concentration are considerably too low. The National Commission on Food Marketing study states that:

> "The wholesale bread baking industry in 1965 consisted of nine large multi-state corporations, three large cooperatives whose members are independent bakers, and a large number of small independent bakers." [20]

They estimate that the twelve major baking companies accounted for 64 percent of bread production in 1965 (one-third by the three major co-

[20] NCFM, *Milling and Baking Industries, op. cit.*, p. 50.

operatives). A recent FTC study estimates that the three largest retail grocery chain stores account for an additional 7 percent or a total of 71 percent for all fifteen.[21] Evans and Walsh estimate that in 1958 local bread market areas averaged between 150 and 300 miles in radius around baking establishments.[22] Therefore, any appraisal of the structure of actual competitive markets requires the inclusion of concentration data for state and local market (SMSA) areas. State concentration data for 1958 are summarized in Table 6-10.

Table 6-10   Bread and Related Products—Share of the Value of Shipments Accounted for by the Four Largest Companies, by State: 1954 and 1958

LEVEL OF CONCENTRATION	Number of States[a]	
	1954	1958
90 and over	1	1
80–89	2	4
70–79	6	6
60–69	7	5
50–59	7	8
40–49	14	14
30–39	9	8
Less than 30	3	3

[a] Includes District of Columbia, but not Alaska and Hawaii.
Source: NCFM, *Organizations and Competitors in the Milling and Baking Industries*, 1966, pp. 52–3.

These data show, for example, that the level of concentration within states increased slightly between 1954 and 1958, and exceeded 50 percent in about one-half of the State markets. In many cases, however, State markets may be too large to be meaningful, and in a limited number of others they may well be too small. It may be worthwhile, therefore, to look at the level of concentration in the industry in individual cities. Table 6-11 shows 4-firm and 8-firm concentration levels in a selected list of 15 large and medium-size cities in 1963. These data show the average level of concentration at the 4-firm level to be about 63 percent.

These data are presented for two purposes, one general and one quite specific. First, they show that despite the rather large number of firms involved in the baking industry throughout the country, competitive markets are relatively small (less than a state in many instances) and

[21] FTC, *Economic Report on the Baking Industry, op. cit.*, p. 41.
[22] Evans and Walsh, *op. cit.*, p. 16.

rather highly concentrated. Second, and much more important, they provide a clear example of the care which must be taken in the uncritical acceptance of national concentration data in the analysis of individual market structures. Here, we noted two major problems. First, the three cooperative organizations (producers of the Sunbeam, Holsum and Bunny brands) are treated as a series of independent entrants. In fact, the producers are "provided complete management services covering all phases of (their) baking operations" [23] These three cooperatives accounted for almost 25 percent of all bread produced in the country. Second, the market is local, not national, and the national data considerably understate actual levels of concentration which determine the type of conduct and performance which prevails.

Table 6-11 Market Concentration in 17 Selected Cities: White Pan Bread: 1963 [a] (as a percent of total sales)

City and State	Four Largest	Eight Largest
Akron, Ohio	59	77
Beaumont, Texas	92	—
Charlotte, North Carolina	73	93
Cincinnati, Ohio[b]	53	79
Denver, Colorado	46	79
Fort Wayne, Indiana	63	77
Long Beach, California	59	78
Memphis, Tennessee	92	99
Milwaukee, Wisconsin	59	75
Minneapolis, Minnesota	39	56
Omaha, Nebraska	76	91
Phoenix, Arizona	78	90
Portland, Oregon	58	76
Providence, Rhode Island	63	84
St. Paul, Minnesota	66	85
Toledo, Ohio[b]	51	74
Washington, D.C.	49	74

[a] Based on estimates of bread purchased in reported cities.
[b] 1964 and 1965 data used where 1963 data were not available.
Source: National Commission on Food Marketing, *Organization and Competition in the Milling and Baking Industries*, 1966, p. 54. These cities were selected by those preparing the above report. All for which data are available and included here.

A brief look at the share of total retail bread sales accounted for by the four and eight largest retail grocery store companies in these same cities shows slightly lower levels of concentration (Table 6-12). Two-thirds of the cities have 4-firm concentration levels over 50 percent. The 8-firm ratios exceed 65 percent in about one-half of the cities.

[23] NCFM, *Milling and Baking Industries, op. cit.*, p. 50.

Table 6-12   Market Shares of the Four and Eight Largest
Grocery Companies in Fifteen Selected Cities, 1963
(as a percent of total bakery products sales)

CITY AND STATE	FOUR LARGEST	EIGHT LARGEST
Akron, Ohio	62.1	71.2
Beaumont, Tex.	41.6	48.5
Charlotte, N.C.	57.0	67.6
Cincinnati, Ohio	49.0	53.0
Denver, Colo.	70.4	75.7
Fort Wayne, Ind.	57.8	79.4
Memphis, Tenn.	28.9	42.8
Milwaukee, Wis.	39.9	47.3
Minneapolis, Minn.	39.3	48.7
Omaha, Nebr.	53.5	61.7
Phoenix, Ariz.	46.6	63.5
Portland, Oregon	35.3	48.5
Providence, R.I.	50.9	65.9
Toledo, Ohio	59.4	67.8
Washington, D.C.	67.3	78.0

Source: NCFM, *Organization and Competition in the Milling
and Baking Industries,* 1966, p. 54.

Excess Capacity   At least one other structural factor should be taken into account prior to our examination of the conduct and performance of firms in the baking industry—the presence of excess capacity. The available evidence in this area suggests that the situation has persisted for some time and that it is nation-wide in impact. Walsh and Evans estimated that excess capacity was quite substantial in 1958, perhaps as high as 50 percent of practical capacity.[24]

The widespread nature of the phenomenon is attested to by the testimony of the President of Continental Baking Company in 1959. At that time, he estimated "that in every city in the country there is far more overcapacity than there is business." [25]

In 1966 the National Commission of Food Marketing pointed out that:

The average plant capacity utilization was 80 percent for the 284 wholesale baking plants reporting this information for 1964 in the Food Commission survey. The South Central region was the lowest with 65 percent utilization and the Northeast was highest with 86 percent utilization.[26]

Excess capacity persists despite (1) a substantial reduction in the number of wholesale baking establishments and (2) a modest increase in

[24] Walsh and Evans, *op. cit.,* p. 65.
[25] *Study of Administered Prices in the Bread Industry, op. cit.,* p. 6789.
[26] NCFM, *Milling and Baking Industries, op. cit.,* p. 55.

the demand. The answer to this apparent contradiction is the rapid improvement made in baking technology. The introduction of continuous batch-mixing processes and higher temperature ovens have resulted in lower production costs, shorter baking times, consequently increased outputs (almost double) from existing physical facilities. As a consequence of these technological changes, new capital expenditures were about $95 million in 1963, roughly the same level as those of 1956.[27]

Market Behavior in the Baking Industry

The use of the term "market behavior" encompasses aspects of both conduct and performance. In the area of conduct we are interested in the extent to which firms in the industry follow policies of "independent" profit maximization as compared with some form of tacit or overt collusion. What are the major dimensions of the competitive strategy of leading firms? We have already looked at one aspect of industry performance—the extent to which long-run excess capacity exists. We might look further at the long-run price-cost relationship and the relationship between relative firm size and profitability. Again, these aspects barely touch on the number of factors which might be taken into account. They do, however, suggest the manner in which such factors may be integrated into an overall appraisal of the strength of competition in a market.

Market Conduct The conduct of firms in an industry takes on particular significance when the structural conditions of the industry depart substantially from those suggested by the competitive model. We have said previously that market conduct is conditioned by the structure of a market. This relationship is not a simple, direct and unvarying one, however. It is affected by a number of factors which assume different weights in different institutional settings. The character of the product, its price, the character of the personnel directing the companies, and past behavior patterns of the companies all introduce unique elements of individuality. In the bread industry as in others it is true that "Anticompetitive acts and practices are most harmful where competitive forces are weak. . . ."[28] Local market concentration is high and apparently getting higher in this industry; therefore, firm conduct becomes extremely important.

The relatively small number of wholesale bakers in any given regional area makes them highly conscious of the actions of their rivals. Moreover, the available evidence indicates that bread purchasers are quite

[27] Bureau of the Census, *1963 Census of Manufactures.*
[28] *The Structure of Food Manufacturing, op. cit.,* p. 150.

aware of price differentials. In such a market—a relatively undifferentiated product and high concentration—it is not surprising that sellers avoid pricing strategies which may have the result of lowering overall bread price levels. One method of achieving price stability in an established market is the adoption of some form of price leadership.

The strength of such agreements vary from market to market. Where competitive conditions are weak the likelihood exists that such arrangements may work. In such situations it is clear that the tacit acceptance of the *status quo* constitutes an optimum competitive solution. This does not necessarily mean individual profit maximization, but a clear awareness of the folly of starting a price war. Where competition is somewhat stronger (concentration lower), more formal arrangements may be resorted to, including overt price conspiracy. While the evidence relating to the presence of tacit arrangements is always weak, there is considerable evidence showing a general pattern of conspiratorial behavior on the part of wholesale baking companies.

Section I of the Sherman Act prohibits attempts to set price through the joint efforts of sellers in a market. Despite this, and the uniform disapproval which the Courts have shown to all such arrangements, a large number of cases involving price conspiracies by bakers have been filed over the past 15 years. All such complaints have involved the *major* bakers in an area. Also, some have included larger retail grocery chains. Two examples will serve to illustrate the range of activities involved and the identity of the alleged culprits.

In October 1967, a criminal complaint was issued by the Department of Justice which alleged that 13 wholesale bakers in the State of Michigan had been engaged in a conspiracy to fix retail and wholesale prices of bread within the state.[29] It further alleged that the bakers conspired to set prices on sales of bread, in supposedly open-bid competition, to schools, hospitals and a variety of public agencies. It is not possible to determine accurately the quantity of sales affected by the alleged agreements. However, the complaint alleged that the companies involved had total bread product sales of $200 million annually in the affected area.

Since such agreements can succeed only if the major firms in the area cooperate, it is not surprising to find that included among the accused were Continental, American, Ward and Campbell-Taggert Associated Bakeries. It is quite common to find regional trade associations listed as defendents in such cases (as in this one) as they often provide the vehicle for the establishment of such agreements. A careful examination of these cases reveals that all or many of the leading national bakers have a substantial history of violating the anticonspiracy laws.

The extent to which these firms engage in their common fight on com-

---

[29] *U.S. and American Bakeries, et. al.* Cr. No. 7613, Western District of Michigan.

petition is illustrated in a case which involved bread sales in the greater Philadelphia metropolitan region.[30] The scope of action of the firms indicated here is interesting. The agreements between the alleged conspirators were designed to raise the prices being charged for so-called "economy breads." Not content with this action in the Philadelphia market, they are accused of entering the York, Pennsylvania market and cutting bread prices to such an extent that as to force a seller in that market who had been selling bread in Philadelphia at a lower price than that charged by the combine to raise his price in the Philadelphia market. These two examples, picked more or less at random, serve to illustrate the type of conduct which has prevailed in the industry in recent years.

In addition to price conspiracy cases, wholesale bakers have been the object of a number of complaints alleging sales activities which have the effect of giving large buyers discounts and other advantages not available to smaller buyers on a proportional basis. Because of the success which large retail grocery chains have had in playing the wholesale bakers one against the other, with threats to transfer their sales to others that will give lower prices, such complaints have met with little success. It is sufficient to point out that the conduct of the major bread producers has been at odds with that which might prevail in a more competitive industry.

Market Performance Reference has been made to the fact that considerable excess capacity existed in the industry in the late 1950s and in 1964–1965. Data presented in the *NCFM Report* shows that capacity utilization varied little between 1960–1961 and 1964–1965. Overall utilization rates increased from 78 percent to 80 percent but varied substantially between regions.[31] These variations changed little through time.

More important, however, in an examination of the impact of the prevalence of excess capacity on market performance is the relationship between rate of utilization and both size of plant and type of firm involved (independent, cooperative, or multistate). In 1960–1961 capacity utilization varied between a low of 75 percent for small plants to 79 percent for large plants. By 1964–1965 the range had doubled from 73 percent to 83 percent with the relative position of different size plants the same.[32]

The increased utilization rates experienced by large multistate bakers were shared by the large bakery chains. Surprisingly, independent bakers showed the greatest increase—from 71 percent to 77 percent. The

[30] *U.S. v. Ward Baking Company, et. al.*, Cr. No. 21123, Eastern District of Pennsylvania.
[31] NCFM, *Milling and Baking Industries, op. cit.*, p. 100.
[32] *Ibid.*

range (13 percentage points) was the same in both years.[33] Capacity utilization is emphasized here as it was with respect to the synthetic rubber industry because it conditions industry performance and is useful in explaining the effect of structural elements upon the retail price and profit performance of the industry.

What has happened with respect to price, costs and profits in the bread industry? We will look first at price-cost relationships for the production of white bread (Table 6-13).

Table 6-13 Estimated Costs, Prices and Spreads
in Production of One Pound Loaf of Bread: 1950–1965
(in cents)

Cost of All Ingredients	Wholesale Spread	Wholesale Price	Retail Spread	Retail Price	Year
4.7	6.7	11.4	2.1	13.5	1950
5.2	7.5	12.7	2.2	14.9	1951
4.9	9.8	12.7	2.4	15.1	1952
5.1	8.1	13.2	2.3	15.5	1953
5.5	8.6	14.1	2.2	16.3	1954
5.4	9.2	14.6	2.2	16.8	1955
5.3	9.7	15.0	2.1	17.1	1956
5.4	9.9	15.3	2.7	18.0	1957
5.3	10.5	15.8	2.7	18.5	1958
5.1	11.3	16.4	2.5	18.9	1959
5.3	11.2	16.5	3.0	19.5	1960
5.4	11.3	16.7	3.3	20.0	1961
5.7	11.1	16.8	3.5	20.3	1962
5.6	11.4	17.0	3.7	20.7	1963
5.6	11.4	17.0	3.7	20.7	1964
5.7	11.4	17.1	3.8	20.9	1965
6.1	12.1	18.2	4.0	22.2	1966

Source: FTC, *Economic Report on the Baking Industry, op. cit.*, p. 117.

Dividing the period since 1950 into three periods plus 1966 shows that distinct patterns exist in each. Between 1950 and 1956, prices rose substantially and rapidly from 13.5 cents per pound to 17.1 cents (by 3.6 cents). Between 1956 and 1960, retail price advanced from 17.1 cents to 19.5 cents to 20.9 cents. During the third period, 1960 to 1965, prices increased by only 1.4 cents. In 1966, however, retail bread prices rose by 1.3 cents per pound alone—the largest single-year increase since 1951.

A detailed examination shows that wholesale bakers obtained almost all (87 percent) of the first period price increase, with the remainder accounted for by increases in the cost of ingredients. Retailers' margins on bread remained almost constant. Between 1956 and 1960 retailer spreads

[33] *Ibid.*

increased from 2.1 cents to 3.0 per pound or by more than one-third.[34] The share of the increase going to the baker declined to 62 percent with 38 percent going to the retailer. In the last period, one-fourth of the increase went to suppliers, 58 percent to retailers, and only 17 percent to the bakers. In 1966, both retail and wholesale prices increased, the wholesalers again obtaining the bulk of the increase; however, suppliers and retailers obtained small shares of the increase. The earlier suggestion that large retailers have become adept at playing wholesale bakers off against each other seems to have been less true in the past few years than it was earlier.

Between 1956 and 1965, the wholesale price of one pound loaves of bread rose about 2.1 cents, while retail bread prices increased about 3.8 cents. How do these price increases compare with changes in the costs of wholesale bakers during this same period? The data show that ingredient costs were relatively stable throughout that period and that about one-third of the cost increase was in plant costs (primarily labor costs) and the remaining two-thirds in selling and delivery costs.[35] These costs typically rise as concentration increases in a market where some degree of product differentiation exists.

Table 6-14   Changes in Wholesale Bakers' Costs: 1956–1965

CLASS OF EXPENSE	Cents per Pound of Bread		PERCENTAGE CHANGE
	1956	1965	
Ingredients	5.56	5.56	0
Plant costs	4.70	5.54	17.9
Selling and Delivery [a]	4.74	6.28	33.6

[a] Does not include stale returns or damaged products which are a reduction from the gross sales.

SOURCE: NAFM, *Organization and Competition in the Milling and Banking Industries*, p. 106.

While the two sets of data are not exactly comparable, they suggest that retail prices of bread increased more than either costs or wholesale prices. As a consequence, the retail margin on bread increased from 2.1 cents per pound in 1956 to 3.8 cents in 1965.

Prior to examining recent changes in profits it is well to provide an answer to a pair of companion questions that are often asked. Do production and selling costs decline as the size of plant increases? Are production and selling expenses lower for large multistate wholesale bakers

---

[34] The terms "margin" and "spread" refer to the difference between the cost of purchasing a product or the materials used in its production and its sale price.

[35] *Ibid.*, Appendix B.

than for members of cooperatives and independents? The answer to both of these questions is no. Large plants and the large multistate firms have the highest level of costs in each comparison. In each case, however, they have the highest level of profits. The reason for this is obviously that they are able to obtain higher prices than the other wholesale bakers have. Greater advertising expenditures explain the bulk of the larger firms' success in obtaining higher prices. Even here, however, considerable differences exist.

Table 6-15   Cost per Pound, by Size of Plant and by Type of Firm: 1964–1965

SIZE OF PLANT	COSTS PER POUND OF BREAD AND BREAD ROLLS
Small	16.36
Medium	16.13
Large	16.57
TYPE OF FIRM	
Independent	16.41
Cooperative	15.99
Multistate	16.51

Source: NCFM, *Organization and Competition in the Milling and Baking Industries*, pp. 134–137.

Although profit data for wholesale bread bakers are fragmentary, they do indicate that: (1) Profit levels declined substantially between 1950 and 1965; (2) Between 1963 and 1967, profits of the largest baking companies recovered to the peak levels achieved during the period; and (3) Smaller bakers' profits continued to decline, reaching all-time lows.

By 1967, the rate of profit of the four largest wholesale bakers had reached a level almost equal to their 1950 level. On the other hand, the "other" bakers' profits were less than one-fourth their 1950 level and less than 30 percent of those of the largest bakers. Their relative position in the industry had slipped substantially.

Many changes have occurred in the bread baking industry. We have characterized the major ones by looking at growth, concentration, capacity utilization, costs, prices and profits. By the careful use of the available data, we can make intelligent and reasonably accurate appraisals of the nature of the major changes that have occurred in the industry, and the effect of these changes upon the vigor of competition.

The bread industry differs substantially from our preceding example in number of firms and level of concentration. In this case we have about 3400 firms in the total industry (1967). However, as we have seen,

Table 6-16   Bread Bakers' Profits After Taxes
As a Percent of Stockholders Investment: 1950–1967

YEAR	FOUR LARGEST	OTHER [a]	RELATIVE RATE [b]
1950	14.1	12.9	91.5
1951	11.1	9.4	85.0
1952	11.6	8.3	71.6
1953	11.7	9.3	79.5
1954	11.9	6.1	51.2
1955	13.7	6.4	46.7
1956	13.6	4.4	42.9
1957	13.3	5.7	42.9
1958	12.2	6.8	55.7
1959	11.8	6.0	50.8
1960	10.3	3.3	32.0
1961	7.3	1.1	15.5
1962	6.6	− 0.1	n.a.
1963	6.2	3.1	50.0
1964	7.3	1.0	13.6
1965	8.6	− 2.5	n.a.
1966	10.3	− 0.1	n.a.
1967	12.7	3.7	29.1

[a] For eight other large bread bakers 1950–1955, for seven in 1956–1957 and four others thereafter.
[b] Profits of "other" as a percent of profits of four largest.
SOURCE: FTC, *Rates of Return for Identical Companies in Selected Manufacturing Industries: 1949–1960, 1955–1965, and 1958–1967.*

baking is not a nation-wide industry. Closer examination shows that in most state and local areas, concentration is typically quite high (Tables 6-10, 6-11, and 6-12).

Perhaps more significant than the level of concentration is the magnitude and direction of change in recent years. Between 1947 and 1967, the share of the four largest companies increased from 16 to 26 percent and the share of the eight largest from 26 to 38 percent. Concurrent with the increase in concentration has come a decrease in the number of firms. The available data do not support a conclusion that this change was prompted by scale considerations.

Just as most of the increase in concentration occurred in the share of the four largest firms, so apparently did profits. In 1950, the profit rate of the smaller bread producers was over 90 percent of that of the four largest. Over the period 1962–67 this same group experienced losses in one-half of the years and relatively low profits in the other three. The effect of the structure changes upon performance is clear.

THE AUTOMOTIVE TIRE INDUSTRY

A recent study by the Federal Trade Commission provides some useful information relating to one of our largest semi-durable consumer good industries. It is an industry which is divided into two distinct sub-markets—original equipment and replacement. Substantially different competitive conditions exist in each sub-market, the effect of these differences is reflected in the competitive behavior of firms in each sub-market.[36]

The discussion of the structure of the market in this industry requires the subdivision of the market into tire manufacturing and tire distribution. This division of the analysis enables one to understand somewhat better the relationships which prevail between the structure of the industry and its performance.

Industry Growth

The growth of the tire industry has obviously paralleled that of the automobile industry in the United States and elsewhere. Between 1925 and 1940, tire shipments remained relatively constant at between 50 and 60 million tires. Over the past twenty-five years, however, shipments of automotive tires almost tripled—from almost 59 million units in 1940 to over 169 million in 1965. Between 1960 and 1965 alone, tire shipments increased by more than 50 million.[37] A similar pattern of industry growth between 1947 and 1967 can be seen from the value of shipments data collected by the Bureau of the Census (Table 6-17).

Despite the rapid growth experienced by the industry, it has experienced a steady decline in the number of firms engaged in the production of automobile tires. The four leading firms in the industry (Goodyear, Firestone, U.S. Rubber, and Goodrich) achieved their dominant position in the industry in its very early stages. However, in these early days there were as many as 500 companies engaged in the production of automotive tires. By 1937, as the result of a variety of factors this number had declined to only 26.[38] In 1945 there were 23 tire producers. But be-

[36] Federal Trade Commission, *Economic Report on the Manufacture and Distribution of Automotive Tires*, 1966. Most of this section is based upon material taken from this study.

[37] *Rubber Industry Facts*, Rubber Manufacturers Association, Inc., pp. 3–5.

[38] These included the development of longer lived tires, the presence of substantial excess capacity (as much as 50 percent in the early 1930s), the entrance of mass distributors into the market, particularly Sears, Roebuck and Co., in the late 1920s

The Automotive Tire Industry 143

Table 6-17 Shipments of Tires and Tires and Tubes:
Selected Years 1947–1965

Year	Tires[a]	Tires and Tubes[b]
1947	d	$1547[b]
1954	d	1997
1958	d	2578[c]
1960	119.6	2844[c]
1963	138.5	2951[c]
1965	169.1	3380[c]
1967	d	3734[c]

[a] Millions of automotive tires shipped.
[b] Value of shipments of tires and tubes
(SIC 3011) in millions of dollars. These
figures are not directly comparable with
the physical output data. They include
the value of inner tube and all types of
industrial and non-automotive tires, as
well as automotive tires.
[c] Revised series (1958).
[d] Not available on comparable basis.
Source: Rubber Manufacturers Association, *Rubber Industry Facts, 1966;* and
the Bureau of the Census, *Census of Manufactures, 1967, Industry Series,* MC
67(2)-30A.

tween 1945 and 1965 an additional nine firms left the industry or discontinued the production of automotive tires. Thus, by 1965, only 14 companies remained in the industry. These data for the period 1940 and
1965 provide an interesting contrast. Tire shipments almost tripled while
the number of producers was cut in half. In their 1939 study, Thorp and
Crowder pointed out that Dun and Bradstreet reported 52 bankruptcies
among tire producers between 1927 and 1934.[39]

General Changes in Concentration Weston's interesting study
of growth by merger provides a rough estimate of the magnitude of the
change in concentration which occurred over the two decades between
1919 and 1939. He estimated that the share of the four largest increased
from about 55 percent to about 77 percent of total industry shipments.[40]
Since 1939, it appears that the level of concentration in the production
of automotive tires and tubes has declined only slightly and remains at
high levels.

and the depression. The result of all of these pressures was a period of intense price
competition starting in about 1927 and lasting for a number of years.
[39] Thorp and Crowder, *op. cit.,* pp. 28–29.
[40] J. F. Weston, *The Role of Mergers in the Growth of Large Firms,* University of
California Press, 1953, p. 41.

Table 6-18   Changes in Concentration in the Production
of Automotive Tires and Tubes: 1935–1967

| | Share of Industry Shipments | |
| | FOUR LARGEST | EIGHT LARGEST |
YEAR	COMPANIES	COMPANIES
1935	80	90
1947	77	90
1954	79	91
1958	71	80
1963	70	89
1967	70	88

Source: Compiled from U.S. Bureau of the
Census, *Concentration Ratios in Manufacturing
Industries,* 1963, Part I; and *Census of Manu-
factures, 1967.* Special Report, *Concentration
Ratios in Manufacturing* MC 67(S)-2.1, p. SR
2–22.

It should be noted that most of the change in concentration has occurred since 1954 and in the share controlled by the four largest producers. Between 1958 and 1963, however, concentration remained relatively
constant.

One problem with the interpretation of these data is that the category
is so broad that it is difficult to analyze the actual state competition in
particular product markets. As a consequence, let us look at the level of
concentration in several markets (replacement and original equipment)
and for different products (passenger, truck and bus tires).

Concentration by Type of Market [41]   Market concentration is
somewhat different in the original and replacement markets. In many
ways, the structure of the *original equipment market* is somewhat sim-
pler. First, only a limited number of firms are engaged in the sale of
tires for the original equipment market. Almost all original equipment
sales (percent of total tire sales) are made by the "Big Four" (U.S. Rubber, Firestone, Goodyear and Goodrich). According to a report which
appeared in 1966, General Tire and Rubber accounted for 5 percent of
original equipment sales to General Motors and 7 percent of sales to
Ford. [42] By the process of simple multiplication it is apparent that the
"Big Four" account for about 95 percent of total original equipment
sales. None of the other smaller producers were able to break into this

---

[41] This and the concentration by product discussion are in terms of physical shipments rather than in terms of value of shipments. The results are slightly different,
at least in the 1958–1962 period covered by the 1966 *FTC Tire Report.*
[42] *Rubber World,* January 1966, p. 61.

market. "Big Four" tire producers accounted for about 83 percent of truck and bus original equipment sales in 1962, up from 78 percent in 1958.[43]

Competition for sales in *the replacement market* is somewhat greater. Here, of course, intercorporate accommodation relationships between firms are considerably less important. It is interesting to note that the replacement market is by far the larger of the two major markets (exports excluded). A brief look at the 1958–1962 period illustrates that, although substantial, the importance of the "Big Four" in the replacement market is somewhat lower than in the original equipment market, although their share increased slightly during the period. In 1962, the four largest tire producers accounted for 66.0 percent of all replacement tire sales, up slightly (1.3 percentage points) from 1958.

Table 6-19 "Big Four" Tire Producers' Share
of Replacement Tire Sales: 1958–1962

YEAR	PERCENT OF TOTAL
1958	64.7
1959	65.6
1960	63.8
1961	65.8
1962	66.0

SOURCE: Computed from Federal Trade Commission, *Economic Report on the Production and Distribution of Automotive Tires,* 1968, Appendix Tables 8 and 12.

In general, it appears that concentration in the automotive tire industry is among the highest in this country. The level of concentration in the original equipment industry, where approximately 95 percent of all sales are accounted for by the 4 largest tire producers, exceeds that in the remainder of the industry. Although the level of concentration is somewhat lower in the replacement market, it is substantial, around 65 percent, and it appeared to increase slightly between 1958 and 1962. This increase corresponds closely to the overall increase in concentration which is shown in the data shown in Table 6-17.

Concentration by Type of Product   As we have seen, there are considerable differences in the levels of concentration in the original equipment and replacement market. A brief examination of the 1958–1962 period will enable us to determine the structure of the two

[43] FTC, *Economic Report on the Manufacture and Distribution of Automotive Tires, op. cit.,* p. 105.

146   *Case Studies in Competition*

major product segments—passenger car tires and truck and bus tires. In terms of physical volume, passenger car shipments constitute the bulk of the total. Truck and bus tires accounted for only 8 to 10 percent of the annual tire shipments between 1958 and 1962. On the other hand, they are important in terms of value of shipments—about 30 percent. The reasons for this are obvious when one reflects on the different size, strength and performance characteristics necessary in the two different classes of product.

What are the different levels of concentration in the manufacture of these two basic classes of products? The answer to this question is contained in Table 6-20.

Table 6-20   "Big Four" Share of Passengar Car and Truck
and Bus Tire Shipments: 1958–1962
(as a percent of total shipments)

Year	Passenger Car		Truck and Bus	
	Total	Replace. Market	Total	Replace. Market
1958	75.9	64.9	71.3	63.5
1959	74.2	63.2	71.8	62.0
1960	74.5	63.9	71.1	62.8
1961	73.8	66.1	72.6	63.6
1962	73.8	66.0	71.9	66.1

Source: Federal Trade Commission, *Economic Report on the Manufacture and Distribution of Automotive Tires*, 1966, pp. 13–14.

These data show that the level of concentration in the sales of truck and bus tires is slightly lower than it is in the passenger car segment of the industry but that the share of sales in the replacement market is about the same for both passenger car tires and for truck and bus tires. It is obvious that the major difference in the control of the four largest tire producers is in the truck and bus original equipment market. One might assume that this is a result of the slightly lower concentration in the production of trucks and busses. Moreover, many of the smaller truck and bus producers do not have as close ties with the four largest tire producers as have the major automobile producers. At the same time it is apparent that between 1958 and 1962 the share of truck and bus replacement tire sales controlled by the four major tire producers did increase.

Shipments of tires have more than tripled in the years since the end of World War II. Between 1947 and 1965 however, tire prices increased by a relatively small amount. The automotive tire wholesale price in 1965 was about 15 percentage points below its postwar high reached in 1958.

Throughout this period, two concurrent changes have taken place. First, the number of tire producers has continued to decline following the trend seen in the late 1920s and 1930s. Because of the vastly different set of economic conditions prevalent in the early period and in the post-1945 period, it is doubtful if the continued decline in number of firms can be attributed to poor economic conditions as was the earlier decline. We will return to this point shortly. Second, between 1947 and 1958 the level of concentration in the industry declined. However, it appears that between 1958 and 1962, the decline leveled off and, in fact, concentration increased slightly. Despite this modest decline, the existing level of concentration in the industry is among the highest which prevail in any segment of United States manufacturing industry. Only four of the other industries with sales of $2 billion or more in 1963 had concentration ratios as high as had tire producers.[44]

Not all segments of the industry are characterized by uniform levels of concentration. Traditionally, concentration has been higher in the original equipment market than it has in the replacement market. Also, it has been slightly higher in the passenger car tire segment of the market than in the truck and bus tire segment. In both cases, differences in the numbers of buyers would seem to be the most persuasive factors accounting for differences in levels of concentration.

The Structure of Tire Distribution

While the production of tires is centralized in the hands of only a few companies, tires are distributed through a large number of outlets and many different methods of sale. This, combined with the varying size of the buyer has resulted in the operation of the industry in a somewhat different manner than might be expected by simply examining the data with respect to tire production. This discussion is restricted to the operation of the replacement market.

Studies of the factors influencing the demand for replacement tires have been sponsored by *Look* magazine.[45] According to their 1965 survey, consumers were most interested in price followed by characteristics related to tire quality. Familiarity with the brand and past satisfaction with the brand were mentioned by only about seven percent of the respondents. It is interesting to note that purchasers of tires manufactured by the largest producers mentioned these factors somewhat more often than was true of purchasers of other brands. It appears, therefore, that

---

[44] The only other industries fitting in this size and concentration size class—over $2 billion in sales and a concentration ratio of 70 percent or more—are cigarettes (SIC 2111), soaps and detergents (SIC 2841), metal cans (SIC 3411) and motor vehicles and parts (SIC 3717).

[45] *Look National Automobile and Tire Surveys.*

tire purchasers are quite price conscious and that the major producers have not been particularly successful in achieving a high level of product differentiation. Further evidence of this can be seen in the distribution of replacement tire sales between manufacturer and private brands. Larger tire producers have generally assumed that tire buyers want quality tires produced by well-known manufacturers. The appeal of private-label sales has been to lower prices.

Channel of Distribution   During the 1920s, replacement tire sales were primarily of first line (best quality) tires and most of them were made through franchised dealers and distributors. In 1926, for example, almost 90 percent of all replacement sales were made in this way.[46] During the depression, greater emphasis was placed upon price and this channel of sale declined substantially in its importance. Following World War II, franchised dealer and distributor sales increased temporarily and then declined steadily.

Table 6-21   Distribution of Replacement Tire Sales
by Channel of Sales: 1929–1964
(percent of replacement sales)

Year	Dealers and Distributors	Oil Companies	Chain and Mail Order	Department Store	Manufacturers' Stores	Other[a]
1929	74.7	0.9	18.4	0.7	4.4	0.9
1930	70.2	3.0	18.0	0.6	7.2	1.0
1935	56.3	12.7	16.6	1.1	12.1	1.2
1940	48.4	16.2	24.0	0.3	9.1	2.0
1946	52.2	18.7	17.0	0.1	9.6	2.4
1950	48.2	24.3	18.2	2.0	7.2	0.1
1955	45.2	25.7	18.5	2.5	8.1	b
1960	41.5	25.8	20.0	1.8	8.4	b
1964	38.8	23.6	20.0	5.0	10.3	b

[a] Direct shipments and cooperative sales.
[b] Included in department store sales.
SOURCE: Federal Trade Commission, *Economic Report on the Manufacture and Distribution of Automotive Tires*, 1966, pp. 115–117.

The only trends of any note to be seen from the data are: (1) the steady and substantial decline in the importance of tire sales through dealers and distributors, (2) the increased importance of oil company service stations as an outlet for replacement tire sales, and (3) the recent increase in tire sales through department store leased departments. In addition, sales through manufacturer-owned outlets have increased steadily since the early 1950s.

[46] W. W. Leigh, *Automotive Tire Sales by Distribution Channels*, University of Akron, 1948.

It appears that tire manufacturers have experienced a substantial change in the type of customer accounting for the bulk of their sales, and as a result of this change are now engaged in sales to a smaller number of larger buyers than was the case prior to World War II. This factor may well explain the relative stability of, and absence of appreciable increase in, tire prices over the period since 1947.

Sales by Type of Brand   Along with the changes which have occurred in the methods by which tires are sold have come changes in the type of product that is sold. The major change that has occurred in this area was in the rise of "private label" brands. A private label is one which carries the name of the retail seller not that of the producer. Private labels have existed in the tire industry since the early 1920s. Sears Roebuck and Co., Montgomery Ward and some of the major oil companies have sold private label tires for more than 40 years. The most rapid expansion in private label (sometimes called distributor label) sales occurred in the early years of the depression. In 1936, private label sales accounted for 22.5 percent of all replacement sales (Table 6-22). By 1941, private label sales rose to 32.5 percent in 1941 and currently they account for about 35 percent of the total.

Private label tire sales are considerably more important in the sale of passenger car tires than of truck and bus tires. Private label sales accounted for about 20.8 percent of truck and bus tire sales compared to 37.0 percent of passenger car sales in 1964. The reason for this substantial difference seems fairly clear. Higher unit costs and the specialized problems of selling to the commercial trucker probably account for these differences. One might add that industrial and commercial tire purchasers, like automobile manufacturers, are interested in price and quality, not in advertising claims and higher prices. Thus, the need for a private label market may not exist.

Table 6-22   Private Label Sales as a Percent of Total Replacement Sales, Selected Years

Year	Total	Passenger Car	Truck and Bus
1936	22.5	a	a
1941	32.5	34.9	18.8
1947	31.8	33.8	21.0
1959	36.1	38.4	19.6
1964	35.1	37.0	20.8

[a]Not available in 1936.
Source: Federal Trade Commission, *Economic Report on the Manufacture & Distribution of Automotive Tires*, 1966, p. 51.

Total private label sales of the nine largest tire producers reached an estimated $359.5 million in 1963, or about 18 percent of total tire sales.[47] This represents an increase of more than $110 million since 1958. A breakdown of such sales by type of customer and size of seller indicates an interesting pattern of relationships between buyers and sellers.

Table 6-23   Private Brand Tire Sales and Market Share,
by Class of Customer, 1958 and 1963
(as percent of total private brand sales of nine largest firms)

| | | *Market Share* | |
CUSTOMER	YEAR	FOUR LARGEST	FIVE THROUGH NINE LARGEST
Dept. store and mail order	1958	38.6	61.4
	1963[a]	27.0	73.0
Major oil company	1958	80.7	19.3
	1963[a]	90.1	9.9
Other	1958	60.5	39.5
	1963[a]	72.2	27.8
Total	1958	59.2	40.8
	1963[a]	62.3	37.7

[a] Figures estimated on the basis of private label sales during the first six months of 1963.
Source: Federal Trade Commission, *Economic Report on the Manufacture and Distribution of Automotive Tires*, 1966, p. 52.

First, the data indicate that while the smaller tire producers have a substantially larger share of the private label sales than of any other market we have examined, their share declined between 1958 and 1963. It is probable that this decline will continue as the "Big Four" continue their invasion of this market. All major producers of tires now produce for the private label market. This is true even of the long-time private label holdout, Firestone, which once claimed that "every Firestone tire carries the Firestone name." However, having entered this market, Firestone became quite aggressive and is now one of the leading private label producers.

Second, the bulk of all private label sales to the major oil companies are under the control of the major tire producers. In 1958, the "Big Four" accounted for 80.7 percent of private label sales to oil companies. By 1963, this figure had risen to 90.1 percent.

Third, the traditional and growing segment of the private label market for the smaller tire producers has been in sales to department stores and mail order companies. Sales to these customers increased from 17.1 percent to 25.0 percent of replacement tire sales between 1946 and 1964.

[47] Pneumatic tire sales totaled about $2.1 billion in 1963.

Major purchasers of private label tires are quite concentrated, however, the level of concentration has declined as the number of significant private label customers has increased (Table 6-24). The decline in concentration on the buying side is simply a reflection of the increase in the number of large private label customers. It is not surprising, however, that there have been no changes in the identity of the major purchasers of private label tires. They include four oil companies (American Oil, Gulf Oil Co., Humble Oil and Refining Co., and Mobil Oil Co.), two mail-order companies (Montgomery Wards and Sears Roebuck), Western Auto Supply Co., and National Cooperative, Inc.

Table 6-24 Concentration of Private Label Purchases From the Nine Largest Tire Producers: 1958 and 1963[a]

Size Class of Purchaser	1958	1963[b]
Four largest	55.0	50.8
Eight largest	77.8	70.6
Twenty largest	96.4	89.8

[a] These nine firms reported a net total of 25 purchasers of private label tires in 1958. This number had increased to 58 by 1963.
[b] Estimated on the basis of sales during first six months of 1963.
Source: FTC, *Economic Report on Production and Distribution of Automotive Tires*, 1966, p. 55.

The Performance of the Industry

While concentration in the production of automotive tires is at a high level, substantial changes have occurred in distribution. The *FTC Report* upon which this section is based suggests that, partially as a result of changes in the distribution system, the performance of the industry is somewhat more competitive than might be anticipated purely on the basis of the structure of tire production.

Ultimately, the question of the desirability of the structure of an industry must be settled in terms of some objective measures of the performance of the industry. Answers must be obtained as to the level of progressivity and profitability of firms in the industry. In highly concentrated industries, one might be interested in the profits of the major firms compared with the other firms. It is only in this way that one may ultimately *confirm* the anticipated results of a particular market structure and changes in a given situation.

The measurement of progressivity is, of course, an extremely difficult and highly technical question. In an industry which has been highly concentrated for some time, it may be more difficult to assess the industry's technical progress and the extent to which it is related to structure. One method is to look at the level of research and development $(R+D)$ expenditures in an industry. On *a priori* grounds, high levels of $R+D$ expenditures relative to sales or some related variable might be used. An examination of these statistics for the tire industry does not indicate that such activities account for a significant portion of industry expenses. Moreover, they appear to be low in comparison with these in other industries with similar levels of concentration.

Profits and Performance Levels   The recent profit experience of leading tire producers and others is available for recent years (Table 6-25). These data show that the profits earned by the four leading firms in the industry have, on the average, exceeded those of the smaller firms in the industry. It would appear that the larger and considerably more integrated firms have been somewhat more successful in offsetting the effects of the low price levels which have prevailed since 1950.

In part, the disparate profit levels are a reflection of the extent to which the large firms are vertically integrated. A portion of the difference, however, probably reflects the high level of concentration which exists in the industry.

What does all of this information mean to students of the economics of the American automotive tire industry? It is not easy to present any complete or definitive answer to that question, but some inferences can be drawn from the data.

First, the level of control which exists in the industry is rather high and after a period of modest decline (prior to 1958) it has begun to increase. Some of this change is a result of merger activity, some a result of interfirm competitive behavior.

Second, the key to the degree of competition in the industry apparently depends upon an increase in the number of large private label sellers. These firms are apparently able to force price concessions from their almost equally large suppliers and to compete in such a way as to produce genuine downward pressure upon the general level of prices. A part of this pressure has been a reduction in the general level of tire quality through time. According to one estimate, premium-tire replacement sales declined from 15 percent in 1953 to 5 percent in 1959. At the same time, second and third line sales increased from 15 percent to 60 percent in the same period.[47] Such a change in product mix produces a general downward pressure of product prices. Assuming some increase in tire quality through time, second line tires in 1959, first line tires in

---

[47] Federal Trade Commission, *Economic Report on the Manufacture and Distribution of Automotive Tires,* 1966, p. 80.

Table 6-25   Rates of Return After Taxes
on Stockholders' Investment of 13 Tire and Tube Producers
and Wholesale Tire Prices: 1954–1967

Year	Four Largest Companies	Other Companies[a]	Wholesale Price Index, Automotive Tires[b]
1954	11.9	4.6	89
1955	15.0	9.4	98
1956	13.2	9.2	102
1957	11.9	7.3	102
1958	10.4	9.3	103
1959	11.4	12.6	94
1960	10.2	6.2	85
1961	9.7	5.3	86
1962	8.6	7.1	86
1963	8.7	5.0	89
1964	10.3	8.1	87
1965	10.9	7.9	88
1966	11.6	10.0	?
1967	10.1	10.9	?

[a] Data only available for nine other companies for 1954 and 1955; for seven companies thereafter.
[b] 1957−1959=100.
Source: Federal Trade Commission, *Report of the FTC on Rates of Return for Identical Companies in Selected Manufacturing Industries,* various issues 1955 through 1968.

1959, and first line tires in 1953 *may* not be greatly different products. Finally, an industry such as this should be kept under more or less continuous review. Any changes in the structure of the industry, either in terms of production or distribution, should bring about prompt examination and action by the appropriate authorities. Certainly, overt actions of the larger firms which are directed at reducing the competitive viability of smaller firms should be dealt with rapidly. The failure to deal with overt anticompetitive conduct simply hastens the departure of smaller producers. Given the apparent lack of any technological necessity for giant firms in the industry, prompt action may provide a real economic benefit. It avoids further reduction in the strength of competition while encouraging economic efficiency.

SUMMARY

This chapter contains a substantial amount of detailed empirical data relating to the overall nature and operation of three important but substantially different industries. They were selected primarily because recent and fairly comprehensive data were available for all three. Quantity of data alone is no insurance that the researcher will be successful in appraising the effects of market changes. Millions are spent annually in the preparation and publication of data by a variety of agencies and firms. In many cases, these data tend to confuse rather than clarify issues. Many instances exist where organizations, usually trade associations, have discontinued the publication of data which could be used to determine the actual nature of the changes which were occurring.

This is not intended as a summary of the factual data included. It is a brief review of the methods and logic employed in reaching conclusions about specific industries. "The structure is the thing" has been the message of this book. The number of firms, their relative size, the presence of entry barriers, changes in product differentiations and related factors define the structure of an industry.

However, they do more than that. Careful examination of available data enable us to detect the ways in which the structural conditions affect the conduct of firms which constitute the relevant market. Conspiracy, discrimination and other anticompetitive behavior can be predicted in some markets with virtually the same degree of certainty that their absence can be expected from competitive market structures. Care must be taken, of course, not to see conduct which doesn't exist. On the other hand, looking at too many trees will surely obscure the nature of the forest. Total information regarding conduct is not available, and much of that which is, is impossible to quantify. Many, if not most, large and important industrial firms go to great lengths to obscure the things they do.

The final factor of importance to be kept in mind, and perhaps the crucial one, is the way in which the industry performs. What has happened to cost-price relationships? What is the pattern of profits in the industry? Do significant differences exist between general profit levels and changes in the profit level of the major firms in the industry when compared to others? If so why?

We have attempted to show how this may be undertaken. In all cases, answers for the above questions are important. In answering them, the discernible relationships between industry structure and performance are stressed. By now it should be apparent that industry performance is not a random variable. It is dependent upon the structure of the industry. Contrary to popular myth, profits don't just happen, nor on the average are they the result of superlative management, rather they depend primarily upon the firm's position in the market. This has always been true in industries not undergoing technological revolutions. Market power determines success. The rest is almost trivial.

7

THE PREVENTION AND
ELIMINATION OF MONOPOLY

[I]n the famous Statute of Monopolies, the Parliament, facing both ways, gave sanction to monopolies already established and prohibited the vesting of new ones. The gentlemen who met in Philadelphia in 1787 were determined that this chapter in English history, which made a number of honorable companies the overlords of domains within the economy, would not be repeated here.[1]

The development of economic thought with respect to the major problems of industrial organization parallels, in many ways, the development of legal thought and judicial interpretation. Prior to the end of the nineteenth century, the monopoly problem was not substantial and certainly not one that received much attention. A number of factors have been suggested as being responsible for bringing about this change in attitude regarding monopoly structure and conduct in the twentieth century. The precise reasons for this change in attitude are not clear. Some view the disappearance of the Western frontier as the basic factor, and with this the change in emphasis from man against the elements to man against man. Others blame the technological developments which necessitated the development of large-scale enterprise and the rise of the giant corporation. Whatever the reasons may be, little attention was paid to the conduct and structure of business prior to the late 1800s. The situation

[1] Walton Hamilton, *The Politics of Industry*, New York, Alfred A. Knopf, 1957, p. 69.

has changed so substantially, however, that such problems are now considered to be a matter of general public concern, and are carried in the popular press as front page items.

Thus far, our attention has been devoted solely to economic problems and to the development of economic thought with respect to the analysis of industry conditions. In this chapter, our attention shifts to an overall view of the development of the law regulating competitive conduct of firm and structure of industries, as well as to a brief discussion of the scope of the present laws. The laws under examination represent our past statutory and judicial response to the economic problems associated with the presence and exercise of monopoly power.

OUR ENGLISH COMMON LAW HERITAGE

The first recorded case which dealt with monopoly conduct was decided in 1599. It involved the legality of a by-law passed by the London tailors' guild in 1571 which attempted to limit the amount of work that could be done by nonguild members. The Court decided that "a rule of such nature as to bring all trade or traffic into the hands of one company, or one person, or to exclude all others, is illegal." In *Darcy v. Allen* (1603) the Court went further and held that royal grants of patent were illegal if they achieved the same end. As Letwin points out, "Darcy's patent was held void on the argument that it violated the right of others to carry on their trade." [2]

It is tempting to assume that these decisions constitute a part of a continuing stream of thought and opinion with respect to the economic and political objections to monopoly. It is not clear, however, that these cases represent such a sentiment or commitment. The period of time encompassing the end of the sixteenth and start of the seventeenth centuries was one of considerable social and economic turmoil in England. The Guild system was rapidly disintegrating. The Crown and Parliament were engaged in a struggle for dominance, or at the very least, in a struggle for the extension of their respective powers. In this context, are the decisions part of an underlying philosophy of broad change in prevailing economic and social thought, or simply isolated actions designed to deal with particular and specific points of irritation? From the evidence, it seems clear that these cases did not represent any widespread aversion to the possession of economic power associated with monopoly positions. They were more a reaction against a particular possessor of that power.

As the common law developed in this area, monopoly positions were

[2] William Letwin, *Law and Economic Policy in America*, New York, Random House, 1965, p. 28.

attacked because they constituted a constraint upon the right of other firms to conduct business. The "sin" of the monopoly grant was, therefore, that it either inhibited entry of new firms or had the effect of eliminating existing firms from the market. Monopoly grants were undesirable because of the damage inflicted upon other firms, not because of any general adverse effect upon the public welfare. Thus, the historical antecedents of our antitrust laws are common law prohibitions against unreasonable contracts and combinations in restraint of trade.

Starting from this common heritage, the treatment of such contracts or conspiracies varied widely between the United States and England. Letwin points out, for example,

> That by 1894 English law on contracts in restraint of trade was not in any important respect an instrument for the maintenance of a competitive economic order . . . , that competition was no longer public policy, or at least that freedom of contract had become a more important end than freedom of trade.[3]

On the other hand, Congress had passed not only the Interstate Commerce Commission Act (1887) but the Sherman Act (1890) which contained strong prohibitions against both contracts and conspiracies in restraint of trade and the presence of monopoly power itself.

THE LAW AND INDUSTRY STRUCTURE

In the 1870s and 1880s considerable attention was devoted to the "trust" problem by the press, labor organizations, and farm groups; sentiment against trusts was strongest in the middle west. The feeling was so strong in Minnesota, for example, that a legislator running as a candidate of the Anti-Monopoly party was elected to the Minnesota legislature in 1873. The major national political parties were slow to give any formal recognition to the public's attitude, however. It was 1888 before either of the two major national party platforms contained antimonopoly planks. The Republican platform of that year proclaimed that:

> We declare our opposition to all combinations of capital, organized in trust or otherwise, to control arbitrarily the condition of trade among our citizens . . .

The Democratic party platform stated:

> Judged by Democratic principles, the interests of the people are betrayed when, by unnecessary taxation, trusts and combinators are permitted to exist . . .

[3] *Ibid.*, pp. 45–46.

Here, too, not all members of Congress were united in their condemnation of the rise of monopoly power which was symbolized by the "trust" problem, despite the fact that widespread large-scale merger activity, with the type of monopoly conduct discussed in Chapter 4, had aroused considerable antibusiness sentiment. It was against this background that the Sherman Act was passed in 1890.

As originally conceived, the Sherman Act was an exceeding simple piece of legislation. The substantive portions of the Act were contained in Sections 1 and 2. They read in part (emphases added):

> *Sec. 1. Every* contract, combination in the form of trust or otherwise, or conspiracy in restraint of trade or commerce among the several States, or with foreign nations, is hereby declared to be illegal . . . *Sec. 2. Every* person who shall monopolize or attempt to monopolize, or combine or conspire with any person or persons to monopolize any part of the trade or commerce among the several States, or with foreign nations, shall be deemed guilty of a misdemeanor . . .

The Sherman Act—Anti-Monopoly Activity   Our experience over the past 100 years demonstrates that the passage of a statute prohibiting a certain act or specific types of conduct does not assure the cessation of the prohibited actions. This is certainly true in the area of antitrust law. The actual effect of the statute depends upon the construction given it by the courts. Early interpretations of the Sherman Act antimonopoly provisions by the Supreme Court demonstrate the validity of this observation.

Few antitrust cases were prosecuted successfully prior to 1911 because of an aversion to such statutes by some members of the Supreme Court, and a deep division of opinion among the others regarding the meaning of the word "every." In the early years, sentiment existed for a liberal interpretation.[4] Both the Standard Oil and American Tobacco cases decided in 1911 represent a clear change in the meaning of the statute as a result of judicial interpretation. In effect, it changed the wording of the statute from "every" to "every unreasonable" act. This "rule of reason" introduced a variety of considerations into all Section 2 cases. Attempts to monopolize, therefore, would have to be evaluated in terms of the company's intent, success in achieving their monopoly position, the absolute size, and the share of the market actually achieved.

In both of the cases referred to above, the companies were broken up into a number of companies. In both cases, however, the companies in question had 90 percent or more of the market. Moreover, their recorded conduct gave clear evidence of an intent to achieve a monopoly posi-

---

[4] For an interesting discussion of the development of the "rule of reason," see Milton Handler, *Antitrust in Perspective*, New York, Columbia University Press, 1957, pp. 3–28.

tion. The same basic standard has been applied in all of the cases decided under Section 2 since that time. Virtually all such cases decided since then have dealt with the reasonableness of the restraint, and the intent of the parties, as well as the actual result. Successes have been few since there is no clear guideline as to the meaning of "monopoly" within the context of the statute.

The impotence of the Sherman Act to deal with present accumulations of economic power is expressed pointedly in the recent *White House Task Force Report on Antitrust Policy*.[5] It states that:

> [A] gap in the law remains. While section 7 of the Clayton Act provides strong protection against the growth of new concentrations of market power in most instances, existing law (the Sherman Act) is inadequate to cope with old ones.[6]

It is worthwhile to point out that no significant cases seeking to reduce or limit existing levels of concentration have been filed under Section 1 of the Sherman Act for at least 20 years.

Antimerger Legislation and Enforcement   Strangely enough, this reluctance of the courts to define situations which did not violate the "rule of reason" was responsible, at least in part, for the first concerted efforts to pass legislation (Cellar-Kefauver amendment to Section 7 of the Clayton Act) aimed at what appeared to be the grossest form of anticompetitive conduct—merger.

Let us look briefly at the history of antimerger legislation. In 1914, the Congress in part as a reaction to what it felt was the failure of the courts to uphold the general prohibitions of the Sherman Act, passed the Clayton Act which made illegal a number of specific forms of conduct which might have the ultimate effect of giving monopoly-like performance. One of these dealt with merger activity. In its original form, Section 7 read:

> No corporation engaged in commerce shall acquire, directly or indirectly, the whole or any part of *the stock or other share* capital of another corporation engaged also in commerce, where the effect of such acquisition may be to substantially lessen competition (38 Stat. 732) between the corporation whose stock is so acquired and the corporation making the acquisition, or to restrain such commerce in any section or community, or tend to create a monopoly of any line of commerce. (emphasis added)

[5] *White House Task Force Report on Antitrust Policy*, July 5, 1968, hereafter referred to as *The Neal Report*, as reported in Bureau of National Affairs, *Antitrust and Trade Regulation Report* No. 411, May 27, 1969. Page references are to the latter source.
[6] *Ibid.*, p. 6.

Despite the intent of the Congress, Section 7 turned out to be a complete and total failure in arresting merger activity. The causes of this were twofold. First, the statute prohibited only the acquisition of stock in competing corporations. It said nothing about the acquisition of the assets of other firms. While this now appears to have been a monumental oversight, it must be remembered that asset acquisition was relatively rare at that time. Second, the decision rendered by the Supreme Court in 1926 made prosecution under the original Section 7 a virtual impossibility. This was an interesting case. Thatcher, the leading producer of glass milk bottles in the United States, had acquired a major competitor through the purchase of a majority of the stock. The Department of Justice filed suit under Section 7 of the Clayton Act. Shortly thereafter, Thatcher acquired the *assets* of the same company alleging the law did not bar the purchase of the assets of competitors only the acquisition of capital stock. Despite the fact that Thatcher's actions were contrary to the spirit (if not the letter) of the law, and the purchase of the assets was made after the complaint had been issued, the Supreme Court upheld the company's position. From that time until 1950, therefore, a company always had the option of evading prosecution by purchasing the assets of a corporation after a complaint was filed against them. As a result of that decision, the statute fell into disuse.

As a result of the Court's action in Thatcher, merger prosecution was only attempted under Section 2 of the Sherman Act. However, the prohibitive standards of monopoly power set under the Sherman Act—intent and the size of market—precluded any substantial number of prosecutions. For 36 years, from 1914 to 1950, merger activity of all types continued almost without check.

In 1950, partially in response to the *inability* of the antitrust agencies to prosecute successfully large mergers which appeared to have a discernible anticompetitive affect short of achieving a complete monopoly position, Congress revised the Clayton Act. As revised, it reads:

> That no corporation engaged in commerce shall acquire directly or indirectly, *the whole or any part of the stock or other share capital* and no corporation subject to the jurisdiction of the Federal Trade Commission shall acquire the *whole or any part of the assets* of another corporation engaged also in commerce, where in any line of commerce in any section of the country, the effect of such acquisition may be substantially to lessen competition, or to tend to create a monopoly. (emphasis added)

Under the revised Section 7, the record of prosecution has been considerably different. In fact, George Stigler, certainly no advocate of expanded antitrust policy, has commented with approval that "The 1950 Merger Act has had a strongly adverse effect upon horizontal mergers by large companies."[7]

---

[7] George Stigler, "The Economic Effects of the Antitrust Laws," *The Journal of Law and Economics*, October 1966, p. 236.

In her excellent review of the first 15 years of enforcement experience under the revised Section 7, Betty Bock noted that the FTC and Antitrust Division filed 170 merger complaints between 1950 and 1965.[8] As Stigler pointed out, one effect of these complaints has been the virtual elimination of horizontal merger activity—the acquisition of direct competitors.

It is interesting to point out the trend in merger activity, prior to and following the passage of the Cellar-Kefauver Amendment (Table 7-1). Here we can see the effectiveness of the revision of our basic and antimerger law in dealing with horizontal mergers. During a period when merger activity was increasing rapidly (from 235 manufacturing and mining acquisitions in 1951 to 2,407 in 1968), the relative importance of horizontal mergers decreased substantially (from 35 percent to 8 percent of the total).[9] The actual number of such mergers remained about the same. By way of comparison, horizontal mergers accounted for 64.3 percent of the total over the 1926–1930 period.[10]

Table 7-1 Distribution of Manufacturing Mergers by Type of Acquisition: 1951–1955 to 1966–1968

Type of Acquisition	Percent of Annual Total			
	1951–1955	1956–1960	1961–1965	1966–1968
Horizontal	35	23	16	8
Vertical	12	15	18	10
Conglomerate	53	62	66	82

Source: FTC, *Economic Report on Corporate Mergers*, October 1969, p. 63.

In summary, it appears that it is only in the area of horizontal merger activity, and even there only since 1950, that the government has made any progress in halting or slowing the pace of increasing concentration. This appears to be the major accomplishment from 80 years of antitrust activity.

LAWS AFFECTING MONOPOLISTIC CONDUCT

Despite, or perhaps because of, the inability or unwillingness of Congress and the courts to come to grips with the basic problems related to

[8] Betty Bock, *Mergers and Markets*, The National Industrial Conference Board, 1966, p. 9.
[9] Federal Trade Commission, *Current Trends in Merger Activity, 1969*, March 1970, p. 9.
[10] Carl Eis, "The 1919–1930 Merger Movement in American Industry," *The Journal of Law and Economics*, October 1969, p. 294.

market structure, they have devoted considerable attention to the area of anticompetitive conduct. These areas include market sharing agreements, price conspiracies, price discrimination, and miscellaneous "unfair" practices.[11] Each of these will be dealt with briefly. Each has a common element: If practiced, it is assumed that the firms involved (because of their market position) are able to inflict injury upon competitors and/or customers because of their actions. The laws which prohibit these activities seek to limit the exercise of monopoly power, not to eliminate the basic cause—the existence of monopoly power. These activities, therefore, constitute part of an unending battle, which cannot be won using the weapons employed in the past.

Market Sharing   If market sharing (perhaps these might be more appropriately called market splitting) arrangements are to be successful, the parties to the agreement, collectively, must be in a position which approximates a monopoly position. Parties to such agreements may adopt one or both of two primary forms of behavior.

First, they may simply agree to a division of the market among themselves, thereby giving each seller (or group of sellers) an area of almost complete dominance. Three sellers, for example, might divide the country into equal parts with each agreeing to respect the privacy and dominance of the others in their respective market areas. Buyers in each sub-market affected by the conspiracy are faced, therefore, with a single monopolistic seller.

A second approach might be an agreement to limit competition in some areas (usually where viable competitors do not exist) but to engage, individually or jointly, in very active competition in areas where producers who are not parties to the agreement attempt to sell. The first type of agreement affects only their customers. The second can be considered as a direct attack on nonmember producers.

Economists generally are antagonistic toward any form of agreement not to compete. Moreover, it runs counter to the judicial interpretation of English common law. It is not surprising, therefore, that one of the earliest cases decided under the Sherman Act found these specific acts to be illegal.[12]

Price Conspiracies   To set Addyston Pipe and Steel in a separate category may constitute an artificial distinction between it and other cases which involve straightforward agreements to set price. The

[11] Unfair trade practice activity, as usually defined, does not bear directly upon the problems of monopoly conduct. The major exception to this is with respect to some forms of advertising activity.

[12] *Addyston Pipe and Steel Company v. United States*, 175 U.S. 211, 1899.

simple price conspiracy case is a direct agreement and does not necessarily involve market sharing or other devices.

A landmark in this area was the Trenton Potteries case which involved an agreement among some 23 corporations, controlling 82 percent of the output of vitreous pottery bathroom fixtures in the United States.[13] In that decision, Justice Stone pointed out that:

> The aim and result of every price-fixing agreement, if effective, is the elimination of one form of competition. The power to fix prices, whether reasonably exercised or not, involves power to control the market and to fix arbitrary and unreasonable prices.[14]

Defendants in this and other cases had maintained that their action was a reasonable one. Justice Stone dismissed this argument quickly:

> The reasonable price fixed today may through economic and business changes become the unreasonable price of tomorrow. . . . Agreements which create such potential power may well be held to be in themselves unreasonable or unlawful restraints, without the necessity of minute inquiring whether a particular price is reasonable or unreasonable.[15]

The final case of consequence in delimiting the illegal types of price conspiracies involved an effort by Socony-Vacuum Oil Company and all other major refiners to "stabilize" price in the Midwest.[16] In this case, the refiners argued that the intent of their efforts was to reduce the sales of "distress" or surplus gasoline. This program involved the purchase of surplus gasoline supplies held by independent refiners which would be unsalable at the market price established by the major refiners. The Court held that:

> Under the Sherman Act a combination formed for the purpose and with the effect of missing, depressing, fixing, pegging or stabilizing the price of a commodity . . . is illegal *per se*. . . .[17]

Such conspiracies have anticompetitive effects if successful. Firms which might otherwise act independently in the sale of their products now act as one, and buyers are faced with a single, often inflexible, price.

Price Discrimination In its simplest form, price discrimination occurs whenever a seller charges different prices to different buyers for

---

[13] *United States v. Trenton Potteries Co.*, 273 U.S. 392, 1927.
[14] *Ibid.*
[15] *Ibid.*
[16] *U.S. v. Socony-Vacuum Oil Company*, 310 U.S. 150, 1940.
[17] *Ibid.*

the same good at the same time. Price discrimination in practice is the recognition that buyers have differing elasticities of demand, and therefore, the firm may maximize its profits by charging different prices to different customers or classes of customers. Sellers practicing price discrimination must be able to classify their customers according to some common characteristic and be able to forestall trade between them. If firms obtaining the lowest price become purchase agents for other firms, a multiple price system cannot be maintained.

Why object to such a system? The answer probably lies in some misguided sense of equity: an assumption that all buyers *should* pay the same price per unit because those buying at a lower price would achieve an *unfair* advantage over their rivals. The latter is a normative social consideration. Economists traditionally concern themselves with questions of a more positive type: Which alternative is most efficient? *not*, Which goal is most desirable.

Section 2 of the Clayton Act as amended by the Robinson-Patman Act (1936) reads in part:

> That it shall be unlawful for any person engaged in commerce . . . to discriminate in price between different purchasers of commodities of like grade or quality. . . .

The Clayton Act contains two basic exceptions to this general prohibition. It allows price discrimination where it is the result of: (1) "differences in the cost of manufacture, sale or delivery" or (2) differences "made in good faith to meet an equally low price of a competitor." In practice, the first of these defenses is seldom used because the FTC has been reluctant to recognize differentials in the cost of production or sale. Moreover, it may act and has acted to limit price differentials if it feels that the differentials are "*unjustly* discriminatory or promotive of monopoly in any line of commerce." In practice, the "good faith" defense has become the only one which a defendent may adopt with any hope of success.

If price discrimination exists, the seller is assumed to have violated the law until *he* proves that his action conforms to one of the permissible forms of discrimination. The reason for this strange behavior is that the sponsors of the act were violently opposed to large and/or chain retail companies. The act was passed, therefore, in the hope that these large retail organizations would be unable to realize cost savings associated with their position as large-scale purchasers.

Discussion of the value of this point of view would involve too much time and space. It is enough to say that the FTC continues to uphold the law with something approaching religious fervor, despite the fact that the effect of its actions has been to raise costs to consumers, and that the legislation runs counter to the efficient operation of the market place.[18]

THE PROMOTION OF MONOPOLY

The record of Congress in its opposition to the existence and expansion of monopoly power is most uneven. There are a number of instances in which it has acted to *increase* monopoly power, or to eliminate the advantages of competition which might have accrued to consumers as a result of the presence of scale advantages in buying.[19] The law with respect to price discrimination is one of these areas. We will now deal with two other exceptions, fair trade laws and export trade associations.[20]

Webb-Pomerene Export Trade Associations   One of the earliest exceptions to our antitrust laws was embodied in the Webb-Pomerene Act (1918). The Webb-Pomerene Act legalized "export-trade associations" and granted immunity to their members from prosecution under the Sherman and Clayton Acts. Companies belonging to such associations were free to (1) set prices, (2) establish sales quotas of members, and (3) agree to the separation or sharing of markets. The limiting factor, however, was that such activities were to be permitted only in transactions which were involved in export trade.

Our brief review of the Sherman Act indicates that such anticompetitive conduct, without some clear congressional exemption, would be illegal. Even here, the exemption is intended to be quite limited. Export trade associations are enjoined to refrain from engaging in activities which would:

> (1) Restrain trade within the United States; (2) Restrain the export trade of any domestic competitor of the association; (3) Artificially or intentionally influence prices within the United States of commodities of the class exported by such associations.[21]

[18] It is interesting to note that *The Neal Report,* pp. 9–10, recommends substantial revisions in Section 2 of the Clayton Act, particularly where the present form and interpretation have the effect of retarding competition.

[19] These exemptions from the antitrust laws ignore regulated industries, agricultural corporations, labor unions and many other areas. The effect of these additional exemptions is not substantially different from the two which are discussed.

[20] These do not exhaust the areas in which Congress has allowed exceptions to our basic antimonopoly prohibitions. The major area not included is the law with respect to the formation and activities of agricultural cooperatives. An exemption for these organizations was permitted in the Capper-Volstead Act (1922). See Clair Wilcox, *Public Policies Toward Business,* 3rd edition, Homewood, Ill., Richard D. Irwin, 1966, pp. 690–692.

[21] Federal Trade Commission, *Economic Report of the Staff on Webb-Pomerene Associations: A 50-year Review,* June 1967, p. 3. This is the only comprehensive study of the problem published in the last 25 years.

Two practical questions exist, aside from the question of whether or not the member companies do or do not adhere to the above rules. First, what is the economic significance of Webb associations in export trade? Second, what is the impact of the Act upon our apparent position as a defender of competition and promoter of free trade throughout the world? [22]

Questions of the economic significance of the act are of two types— what is the magnitude of Webb assisted sales, and what types of products dominate association sales?

The FTC *Report* analyzes the activities of Webb associations in the period 1958–1962. The most common activity of these associations was the establishment of prices. The report shows that 19 of the 23 active associations in 1962 listed pricing as *one* of their functions.

The data submitted to the FTC indicated that between 1958 and 1962 exports assisted in any manner by an association averaged 2.4 percent of the value of United States exports (p. 36). These exports were limited to a narrow line of goods. The largest was motion picture and television films—almost 60 percent of the total. The next largest group included sulphur, carbon black, phosphate and potash—about 27 percent of the total. Thus, these two classes of products accounted for seven-eights of the dollar value of Webb association exports. It would seem, therefore, that association-assisted exports are relatively small in terms of total United States export trade, and moreover, that they are limited to a small variety of products.

The second major question is that of the apparent contradiction involved in our espousal of a domestic antimonopoly policy and a world free-trade program on the one hand, with our continued support of Webb-Pomerene associations on the other. Our advocacy of this program is more unusual given the apparent movement away from such cartel arrangements by the Common Market.

The FTC *Report* concludes by suggesting that the law be amended for at least two reasons.

First: "A combination of established administrative precedents as well as changing conditions in the world trade provide a basis for recommending that the Congress clarify its intent with respect to the Webb-Pomerene Act. *In particular, it is recommended that Webb-Pomerene exemptions be limited to firms that can demonstrate need.* To amend the

---

[22] We will ignore the question of whether or not it has been successful in promoting the export trade of smaller firms. House Judiciary Report No. 1118, 64th Congress, Second Session, points out, "our large enterprises may be able to stand such expenses alone, but our smaller producers and manufacturers cannot" (p. 4). The export trade association was intended to be a joint sales agency for smaller firms. The law does not forbid large firms from joining such associations. The FTC *Report* shows, however, that small firms have not participated widely in the formation or operation of export trade associations.

law in this manner would fit into the current foreign economic policy of the major world trading nations." (emphasis added)

Second: "The law, as it stands, appears to require the Justice Department or the Federal Trade Commission to establish actual anticompetitive effects before associations can be required to modify their activities or to disband entirely. . . ."

"Since experience indicates that firms most prone to seek Webb exemption belong to such industries, it would appear justified that probable domestic effects on competition be more specifically considered as a matter determining the acceptability of any registration." [23]

Fair Trade Laws The term "fair" trade is a misnomer which has been applied to vertical price fixing agreements entered into by manufacturers, or wholesalers and retailers. They refer to the practice of resale-price maintenance. Once again the Federal laws in the area grant immunity from prosecution to firms engaged in this form of price fixing.

> The Tydings-Miller amendment of 1937, modifying the Sherman Antitrust Act and limiting application of the Federal Trade Commission Act accordingly, removed the bar of illegality to the making of minimum resale maintenance contracts covering commodities sold in interstate commerce if they were resold in a State where such contracts had been legalized [by the State legislature] with respect to intrastate sales.[24]

These exemptions apply only to the sale of trademarked or branded products sold in "open" competition. The theory of such laws is that producers of such products have a proprietary right which extends past the point at which they sell the product and title of the physical product passes to another, and that irrespective of the identity of the actual local seller of the product, the consumer purchases "x" brand. We will ignore the merits of this argument, since it is basically one of social desire and legal definitions, and proceed to the actual operation of these statutes.[25]

Prior to the passage of the Miller-Tydings Act, courts had systematically invalidated resale price agreements. They were unimpressed by the necessity of such a law to maintain the brand-name and/or goodwill of the manufacturers. The courts pointed out that vertical price-fixing agreements between a producer and a number of retailers restrained

---

[23] *FTC Report on Webb-Pomerene Associations, op. cit.*, p. 70.
[24] FTC, *Report of the FTC on Resale Price Maintenance*, December 1945, p. xxvii.
[25] The scope of the basic Act was extended in 1952, with the passage of the McGuire Act to cover non-signers as well as signers. This means that if a state has a fair trade law with non-signers clause but only one firm in a state enters into a resale price maintenance agreement with a manufacturer, all sellers in that state are bound by the terms of that agreement, at least with respect to price.

price competition as effectively as any horizontal agreement between competitors.

Those promoting state and national fair trade laws are commonly moved by a desire to avoid the consequences of existing in a competitive market. They aim, also, at firms which engage in "loss leader" advertising—the advertising of a well-known item at a loss which may suggest similar reductions on other products advertized. The unfortunate part of such agreements is that they strike:

> Not only at promotional price cutting, but at *all* price reductions which pass to the consumer the economies of competitive distribution.[26]

The *Report of the Attorney General's National Committee to Study the Antitrust Laws* went on to point out that fair trade pricing

> When used as a device for relieving distributors from the rigors of price competition is at odds with the most elementary principles of a dynamic free enterprise system . . . The throttling of price competitors in the process of distribution that attends "fair trade" pricing is, in our opinion, a deplorable yet inevitable concomitant of federal exemptive laws.[27]

With respect to such exemption the Report's conclusion is both accurate and comprehensive. Moreover, it introduces what most economists feel are undesirable institutional impediments into the operations of what otherwise would be *freer, more competitive* markets.

The Antitrust Agencies   In this summary examination of the major characteristics and goals of the antitrust laws, one final area deserves some mention—the agencies which are given the responsibility of enforcing these laws. Of particular interest here is the approach and areas of responsibility of the Antitrust Division of the Department of Justice, and the Federal Trade Commission. We will deal with the latter first.

In most cases, there is a relatively clear line of demarcation between the activities of the two agencies. The Antitrust Division is given sole responsibility for the enforcement of the Sherman Act. In addition, it is given joint responsibility for the enforcement of Section 7 of the Clayton Act. This latter activity is the cause of much confusion and considerable ill will between the two agencies. At times there is active competition to initiate a case. In other instances, it is used as an excuse for the failure of either to take any action.

The Federal Trade Commission is given jurisdiction over the enforce-

<hr>

[26] *Report of the Attorney General's National Committee to Study the Antitrust Laws*, May 1955, p. 154.
[27] *Ibid.*, p. 155.

ment of the Clayton Act, particularly Sections 2, 3, 7 and 8, and the
Federal Trade Commission Act, particularly Section 5. If one was to
make a distinction between the activities of the two agencies, it could
be argued that the Antitrust Division is almost exclusively engaged in
antimonopoly areas. On the other hand, the FTC is engaged in some antimonopoly activities, but considerably more of its time is spent in actions which involve deceptive practices such as false product claims, in-
accurate advertising and the like.

The major difference in the approach of the agencies, particularly in
the last 15 to 20 years, is one of style. The Antitrust Division has generally been interested in the case-by-case approach to the solution of monopoly problems. It has tended to view each activity in isolation rather
than to deal with the problem as endemic to the industry or a broad
sector of the economy. The major exception to this general categoriza-
tion is in some of the cases involving price conspiracies. Even here,
however, the cases are dealt with as individual and unique actions.

At times, the FTC uses a similar approach; however, a substantial
portion of its efforts have been directed at what it refers to as the industry-wide approach to problems. Such an approach is equally applicable
to merger activity or some form of deceptive practice. It is not surprising to find, therefore, that the FTC Bureau of Economics has produced
more than 100 studies in the past 50 years which deal with (1) problems
common to members of an industry, or (2) actions which may allow anticompetitive performance in the production or sale of products in broad
sectors of the economy.[28] The industry-wide approach tends to produce a
more even-handed approach to all firms in a particular area.

As a part of their industry-wide approach, the Commission conducts
and sponsors a number of meetings and conferences which seek to provide information or assist in the development of solutions to problems
which beset all members of an industry. This difference in approach on
the part of the FTC is potentially of great value. In practice, however,
some argue that the agency has failed to keep abreast of the needs of
the public, and fails to carry through its great promise, and potential. As
a consequence, considerable dissatisfaction exists with respect to its activities.

Excerpts from three different reports suggest the sources and magnitude of dissatisfaction with the Commission's performance.

In 1949, the Task Force of the Hoover Commission said:

> As the years have progressed, the Commission has become immersed in
> a multitude of petty problems . . . The Commission has largely become a
> passive judicial agency, waiting for cases to come up to its docket. . . .
> The Commission has long been guilty of prosecuting the trivial and tech-

[28] Stanley E. Boyle, "Economic Reports and the Federal Trade Commission," *Federal Bar Journal,* Fall 1964, pp. 489–510.

nical offenses and of failing to confine these dockets to cases of public importance.[29]

In 1965, Professor Carl Auerbach reported in a study conducted for the Administrative Conference of the United States that "the important question is whether the Commission has a system of priorities by which it is guided in discharging all the tasks entrusted to it by Congress. To date, the answer is no." [30]

In 1969, the now famous Nader Report on the FTC stated:

> The Federal Trade Commissions failure to perform its enforcement duties properly under the existing law has several aspects. For one thing, there has been a general decline of formal enforcement activity and an unwise shift toward greater reliance on "voluntary" enforcement tools. Even worse, compliance practices have become almost entirely voluntary. Finally, all enforcement programs are vitiated by excessive delays.[31]

When one examines the general quality of the appointments to the Commission, one well might wonder how it has managed to do as well as it has; for even with these shortcomings, the FTC has proved a distinct asset. Without it, things very probably would be much worse than they are now.

SUMMARY

This has been a brief exploration of the goals of each of the major pieces of antitrust legislation, as well as its ultimate impact. Our purpose has been threefold. First, to review the actions and goals of the Congress and the courts, which seek to limit the accumulation of monopoly power, and to forestall the exercise of it once obtained. Second, to show briefly the direction antitrust enforcement has taken, given the statutory framework and judicial interpretation within which the agencies must work. Finally, we have looked at the nature and significance of some of the major exemptions from the Sherman, Clayton, and FTC Acts.

The record in the first of these areas is most disheartening to contemplate. Although the Sherman Act was intended to limit the accumulation of monopoly, we can only conclude that Congress and the courts have

[29] *Hoover Commission Report*, 1949, pp. 125, 128.
[30] Carl Auerbach, "The Federal Trade Commission," *Minnesota Law Review*, 1965.
[31] Edward Cox, Robert Fellmeth, and John Schulz, "The Consumer on The Federal Trade Commission" reprinted in *Congressional Record*, January 22, 1969, p. 375.

neither the will nor the stomach to attempt to maintain or increase the levels of competition in our economy. All available empirical studies show little or no correlation between actual firm sizes and those necessary to achieve available scale economies. Actual plant and firm sizes in concentrated industries far exceed those required by technological considerations.

It is tempting to throw the burden for this, as well as all of our other antitrust ills, upon Congress. In this instance, however, the courts must bear a primary responsibility for this tragic condition. While they have taken the lead in the application of revised Section 7 of the Clayton Act since about 1955, they have failed completely to define a legal standard of monopoly power which can be considered realistic from an economic point of view.

The courts, on the other hand, have been unfailing in their application of the law in areas where price and market sharing agreements exist. Unless overruled, as they have been on occasion by the Congress, they have struck down *all* price fixing conspiracies irrespective of the relationship between the parties to the conspiracy—competitors, buyers and sellers or any combination of them. With the exception of some recent decisions, particularly since 1950, many of these have been empty victories. The same firms have been charged repeatedly with the same, or similar, offenses. More often than not, the fact that they have repeated convictions has failed to diminish their conspiratorial zeal.

Only in the antimerger field do both Congress and the Courts get positive marks. Even here, however, it is apparent that their action has been a function of the relative ease of forbidding the consummation of a merger compared with the problem involved in separating the assets of two or more corporations once a merger has occurred.

Because of the factors mentioned above, it is not surprising to find that the antitrust agencies have been vigorous in pursuing members of price conspiracies and companies engaged in merger activity where the anticompetitive effects are relatively clear. Little or no effort has been devoted to the prosecution of monopoly cases in the past 10 years. Two important monopolization cases, one involving the production of diesel locomotives and the other involving intercity buses, were dropped by the Department of Justice in recent years. In both cases, a single company (General Motors) controlled more than 90 percent of the market.

Our final area of interest, that of antitrust exemption, is difficult to appraise. If one were to simply count pieces of legislation, it would appear that the exemptions are more numerous than the inclusions. Laws relating to resale-price maintenance, export trade associations, sales below cost, price discrimination and the like, are designed to exempt firms in essentially competitive areas from the desirable consequences (from society's point of view) of competition.

In almost every case, Congress has chosen to grant additional exemptions rather than to move toward the elimination of all exemptions. If continued to its logical extreme, this policy ultimately may succeed in making competitive conditions in all markets as bad as those in the worst. This is clearly the path of least resistance. One purpose of this book has been to attempt to change the direction of this movement. We have assumed that an increase in knowledge of the consequences of the development of anticompetitive structures and conduct in markets is the first step toward their systematic elimination. In this case, as in all others, the only goals worth seeking are those which are not capable of easy attainment.

SUGGESTED REFERENCES

General Texts

Bain, Joe S., *Industrial Organization*, 2d edition. New York, John Wiley & Sons, Inc., 1968.

Business Concentration and Price Policy. New York, National Bureau of Economic Research, 1955.

Edwards, Corwin D., *Control of Cartels and Monopolies*. Dobbs Ferry, N.Y., Oceana Publications, Inc., 1967.

Leonard, William N., *Business Size, Market Power, and Public Policy*. New York, Thomas Y. Crowell Company, 1969.

McGee, John S., *In Defense of Industrial Concentration*. New York, Frederick A. Praeger, Inc., 1971.

Mueller, Willard F., *A Primer on Monopoly and Competition*. New York, Random House, Inc., 1970.

Needham, Douglas, *Economic Analysis and Industrial Structure*. New York, Holt, Rinehart and Winston, Inc., 1969.

Nutter, G. Warren, and Henry Einhorn, *Enterprise Monopoly in the United States: 1899–1958*. New York, Columbia University Press, 1969.

Sheppard, William G., *Market Power and Economic Welfare*. New York, Random House, Inc., 1970.

Stigler, George J., *The Organization of Industry*. Homewood, Ill., Richard D. Irwin, Inc., 1968.

173

Specific Books

Bain, Joe S., *Barriers to New Competition: Their Character and Consequences in Manufacturing Industries.* Cambridge, Mass., Harvard University Press, 1956.

Dewey, Donald, *The Theory of Imperfect Competition: A Radical Reconstruction.* New York, Columbia University Press, 1969.

Gort, Michael, *Diversification and Integration in American Industry.* Princeton, N.J., National Bureau of Economic Research, 1962.

Markham, Jesse, and Gustav Papanek, *Industrial Organization and Economic Development: In Honor of E. S. Mason.* Boston, Mass., Houghton Mifflin Company, 1970.

Narver, John C., *Conglomerate Mergers and Market Competition.* Berkeley, Calif., University of California Press, 1967.

Industry Case Studies

Conant, Michael, *Antitrust in the Motion Picture Industry.* Berkeley, Calif., University of California Press, 1960.

Harman, Alvin J., *The International Computer Industry: Innovation and Comparative Advantage.* Cambridge, Mass., Harvard University Press, 1971.

Federal Trade Commission, *Report on the Manufacture and Distribution of Automotive Tires.* Washington, D.C., U.S. Government Printing Office, March 1966.

Federal Trade Commission. *Report on Mergers and Vertical Integration in the Cement Industry.* Washington, D.C., U.S. Government Printing Office.

Federal Trade Commission, *Report on the Structure of Food Manufacturing,* Technical Study No. 8. Washington, D.C., U.S. Government Printing Office, June 1966.

Markham, J. W., *Competition in the Rayon Industry.* Cambridge, Mass., Harvard University Press, 1952.

Mead, Walter J., *Competition and Oligopsony in the Douglas-Fir Lumber Industry.* Berkeley, Calif., University of California Press, 1966.

Weiss, Leonard W., *Case Studies in American Industry.* New York, John Wiley & Sons, Inc., 1967.

INDEX

176   *Index*

Baking industry (*continued*)
performance, 137-142
structure, 129-131
Barriers to entry, 6, 29, 58, 61, 70-71, 117-118, 123
Barriers to New Competition, 53, 67
Berle, Adolph, 32
Bids, 81-82
Blair, John M., 46-47
Boyle, Stanley E., 37, 49, 50, 59, 81, 97, 100, 108, 120, 169
Brand-name, 167
Bureau of the Census, 3, 21, 27, 103, 113, 129, 131, 142
Bureau of Old Age and Survivors Insurance, 22
Business concentration (*see* Concentration)
Buyers, industrial, 11

Capital intensity, 12
Cartel, 81-82
Celler-Kefauver Antimerger Act, 159, 161
Census of Manufactures, 4, 21, 26, 50, 108, 111, 113
Cigarette industry, 63, 89-92
Clayton Antitrust Act, 13, 159-160, 164-165, 168-171
Clorox, 6, 57, 71
Collins, N. R., 32, 33, 104
Collusion, 7, 9, 11, 80-84
Competition
government poling toward, 10
nonprice, 11-12
perfect, 1, 2, 10
standard, 7, 25
Concentration, 24, 31-32, 34, 43
definition, 25
degree, 5
general, 29-31
high, 37
index, 105
industry, 27, 36-38
level, 52, 102
measurement, 26
overall, 17-18, 25, 29
plant, 47-48

ratios, 27-28, 30, 36-37, 108
results, 29, 38
specific, 28-31
trends, 31, 40, 42-43
weighted, 105-106
Conduct, 6, 8
Conglomerate enterprise and mergers (*see* Diversification)
Congress, 17, 23
Construction, 14
Consumer goods, 41, 50-51, 62, 72-73, 84, 87-88, 92, 115
Consumer Reports, 55
Corporations, 16-17, 32-33
Cost-price differential, 7
Current Trends in Merger Activity, 22

Darcy v. Allen, 156
Dealership (*see* Franchising)
Democracy, 30
Dewing, A. W., 46, 100
Dirlam, Joel, 58
Diversification, 28, 30
Divisional reporting, 98
Dominant firm, 59, 79-80
Drug industry, 62
DuPont, 55

Early, James S., 59
Economic concentration (*see* Concentration)
Economic power, 18, 26, 30, 43, 103, 154, 156-158, 162, 165, 171
Economic Report on Corporate Mergers, 34
Economies of scale, 43-44, 46, 71-72
Electrical conspiracy, 81, 83
Employment, 14-15, 18
Evans, B. M., 128-129, 132, 134
Excess capacity, 116-117
Export trade, 165-166

Falero, Frank, 101
Fair trade laws, 9, 83, 167-168
Federal Trade Commission (FTC), 2, 21, 142, 167-168, 170

178   *Index*

Performance, 6-9, 12, 66, 93-98, 101-102, 117, 153-154
Plant size, 43-45
Potential entrant, 6, 69-70
Preston, Lee E., 32, 104, 114
Price
  discrimination, 6-7, 58, 163-164
  fixing, 167
  leadership, 78-79
  policy, 6, 75-76
  variability, 75-76
Producer goods, 41, 50-51, 62, 72-73, 84, 87-88, 92, 115
Product, 4, 7, 22
Product differentiation, 5, 12, 51, 53-73, 76-77, 87, 116, 118
Production capacity, 8
Production costs, 43-44
Profits, 95-101, 103-106, 153-154
Proprietorships, 16
Purex, 6

Quarterly Financial Report for Manufacturing Corporations, 21-22

Regulation, 18, 30
Resale price maintenance (*see* Fair trade laws)
Reid, S. R., 100
Report on Food Manufacturing, 105
Risk, 96-97
Robinson-Patman Act, 9, 164
Rule of reason, 157-159

Saving, T. R., 46-47
Scale economies, 114-115
Schwartzman, D., 110-111, 127
Scitovsky, Tibor, 56
Section 7 (of Clayton Antitrust Act), 159-160
Sheppard, William G., 53

Sherman Antitrust Act, 9, 157-160, 162-163, 165, 167-168, 170
Size distribution, 16-17, 25, 33-35, 38, 86
Socony-Vacuum Oil Co., 163
Standard Corporation Record, 20
Standard Oil, 158
Standard and Poors' Industrial Reports, 20
Statistics of Income, 21
Stigler, George J., 45, 160
Stocking, Collis A., 55
Structure, 5-6, 8, 24
Survivor technique, 45-47
Smith, Caleb A., 44
Sorensen, Robert L., 49, 108

Technology, 12-14, 16, 43, 48, 50
Telser, Lester, 89, 114
Trade journals, 20
Trust, 31, 158
Tydings-Miller Act (*see* Miller-Tydings Act)

Unionism, 112
United States Steel Corporation, 79

Value of shipments, 38
Vertical integration, 26

Wage
  levels, 109-110, 112, 114
  payments, 15
  policy, 110-111
Webb-Pomerene Act, 165-167
Weighted concentration index, 112
Weiss, L., 107, 111-112
Western Union, 1
White House Task Force on Antitrust Policy, 159
Walsh, Richard G., 128-129, 132, 134